D0197847

First Advice:
Don't use $ as book marks!
Love from Mom
XMas 2015

THE EARLY INVESTOR

THE EARLY INVESTOR

How Teens & Young Adults Can Become Wealthy

BY MICHAEL W ZISA

ISBN: 1492105007
ISBN 13: 9781492105008
Library of Congress Control Number: 2013915525
CreateSpace Independent Publishing Platform
North Charleston, South Carolina

This book is dedicated to all of my past, present, and future Investment Management and Wealth Management students. Without all of you, this book would not have been possible. Special thanks to everyone who volunteered to share their thoughts in 'The Early Investor'.

The Early Investor was written with all the love and support from my wife, Kim, and my three sons Rob, Jack, and Kyle.

TABLE OF CONTENTS

FORWARD #1

The student's classic question: "When am I ever going to use this stuff?!" Generations of middle school, high school, and even college students have grappled with the idea that the knowledge they gain in school lacks real-world importance. In response to this claim, educator Mike Zisa introduces *The Early Investor*, exploring an undeniably relevant topic for today's youth-*money*! As both a high school business teacher and a financial advisor, Mr. Zisa combines his educational ability and financial expertise to superbly explain various topics dealing with money management. He explores subjects from compound interest to asset allocation to retirement plans, maintaining a friendly and personal tone throughout. *The Early Investor* has the information of a textbook without all the boring formalities. This easy, yet valuable read will keep your interest and grant you the tools that you need to build your wealth for years to come.

-Jacob Wachspress, High School Student

FORWARD #2

We go to school for 12 years. We sit in classrooms for 2,160 days. We have graduation requirements in Science, Math, English, and History. We have passed the requirements that schools lay out for us. But what have we really learned? Ultimately, how prepared are we for the real world?

I can fire off dates of important battles; I can solve for 'x'; I can analyze an English poem, and I can balance chemical equations. We all can. But ask me how to begin investing to become wealthy, how to save for retirement, or how to decide between investments, and I've got nothing. Many of us know what we want to do with the rest of our lives already, and many of us are still trying to figure it out. But one thing is certain: learning does not stop in school. There comes a point when we have to start taking initiative and learn for ourselves. This book is that initiative; this book is your school when it comes to investing.

-Katie Denshaw, High School Student

FORWARD #3

A well-known National Football League player once said, "We get one opportunity in life to do whatever you are going to do, to lay your foundation and make whatever mark you are going to make. Whatever legacy you are going to make, leave your legacy". The easy choice is to not take the time to learn about investing. Instead, you decide to just sit back and hope things work out just the way you want. Investing may not seem that important to you now, or maybe it is important to you, but you are skeptical. I assure you, however, that the earlier you learn about investing, the stronger you will be financially when you are older.

I am a believer that you can only influence others through teaching if you have experience in the subject matter. You have to have been a part of the industry to see what wrong decisions can cause, and to have accomplished the successful skills and knowledge that you pass on. There are many speakers who tell you how to make money--do this, do that, invest here--, but how many of these experts ever really follow their own philosophy. With experience, a person only really requires one trait--the ability to connect to and understand those being taught. My first business course I ever took in high school was taught by a teacher who fit the above description. The name Mr. Zisa may sound familiar to you since he is the author of this book! People ask me all the time why I am so excited to be a part of '*The Early Investor*'. The answer is very simple. I believe that others deserve the ability to benefit as much from this book and its author as I have throughout my high school years.

Any thought that you will not be able to learn and understand the material within this book is truly misguided. I have had many teachers throughout my educational career and can truthfully say that Mr. Zisa is unique in his ability to deliver complicated material to others. Too often we as learners are left without substance when reading information on finance or economics and thus fail to have any sort of connection with the concepts. This book not only breaks down topics to a level where you can thoroughly understand it, but Mr. Zisa is also able to add flare to something that may seem bland and boring on the surface. The beauty of the book is that it is a powerful tool for all ages. It can establish a base for a young teen or young adult and sharpen older generations' investment techniques.

Investing at a young age is not a hobby. Investing when you are young is an incredible advantage. As a former high school athlete and honor roll student, I recognize that even the slightest edge can make a difference in life. You would be surprised at the vast number of wealth available to those who make the effort to push through basic, yet vital, lessons. I can say that I plan to read every piece of literature for my finance classes and receive top grades throughout my college years, but without that initial effort all I will have is a big dream and a small wallet. As I said previously, my best advice I could give about this book is to absorb as much as you can.

On a personal level, one of my issues when I was in high school was that I did not have enough money to invest as a 9th grader. However, I realized that you do not need thousands of dollars to begin investing. Accumulating great wealth almost always begins with small amounts of cash. My first investment, as basic as it may sound, was twenty dollars into a savings account in order to carry the required minimum balance. The interest I received on this investment was close to nothing, but it still remains better than placing my money under my pillow. Why not let your cash earn *more* money?

The point I would like to make is that we all want to become wealthy at some point in our lives. One of the major problems that we face, myself included, is the inability to stop watching television or checking the most recent posts on Twitter, Facebook, or even Google+. Sure it is easy to put down this book and pick up a remote. Furthermore, it is much easier to wait for someone to give us money than to go out and find a job. However, when has anything in life been easy? My challenge to you is to finish this book, wake up the next morning and, as the late John Wooden once said "Make today your masterpiece". I understand that I sound like a relentless parent, but I need to stress my point because like many people in our country, I was the one stuck on the couch. You have already made one of the best decisions of your life by deciding to pick up this book, so why stop now? Finish it and reap the benefits of what is inside. Trust me! The joke will be on those who ignored the value of knowledge and information shared in "The Early Investor". The journey of life is filled with many challenges and obstacles and this book will help you navigate through one of the most important parts of your trip. Enjoy!

-Kale Pasch, University of Pittsburgh

CHAPTER ONE

WHAT IS INVESTING?

$1 million? $2 million? $10 million?! How much money do you need to be considered wealthy? Most of us would love to become wealthy. Imagine for a moment having a worry-free life full of luxury, travel, and peace of mind. Although being a wealthy individual can have different meanings to different people, monetary wealth can certainly prove to be a worthwhile goal in your life. Maybe money cannot buy happiness, but it sure can help you live the way you want and need. So how do you create wealth? And how do you begin? That is why you are reading this book! However, you should first understand that developing good spending habits will prove to be a worthwhile endeavor on your roadmap to financial success.

As a teenager, you probably are not interested in making a lot of money right now. However, you are also very young. I will show you throughout 'The Early Investor' that investing early in life will put you in a great position on your quest to becoming wealthy. When we refer to investing, we are not talking about saving. There is quite a difference between investing and saving and, although subtle, it is important to distinguish between the two before discussing the topics in this book.

Saving is simply putting your money in accounts such as savings, checking, or money-market accounts at an FDIC (Federal Deposit Insurance

Corporation) insured institution such as a bank. It may also include cash investments such as short-term CDs (Certificate of Deposits) or even United States Savings Bonds. We will learn more about these savings vehicles and investments in future chapters. Savings also means that your money is extremely safe and can be accessed quickly and easily. A word often used that defines the ability to convert any asset (something you own) into accessible cash quickly and easily is *liquidity*.

Investing, on the other hand, is the process of using your money to buy assets such as stocks, bonds, real estate, and other investments that will grow in value over a longer period of time for the purpose of becoming wealthy and having enough money to retire and do the things you want later in life. Contrary to saving your money, investing does carry *risk*. Risk can be defined as the unexpected loss you incur in a specific investment. Risk includes the possibility of losing some or all of the original investment. While saving your money can certainly produce money for you, investing your money has historically been the better performer over longer periods of time.

THE INCREDIBLE POWER OF COMPOUNDING

One of the greatest mathematical discoveries of our time is *compounding*. Compounding is when your earnings from your savings and investments create additional earnings. In other words, compounding is when your earnings generate earnings. The more earnings you create and keep working for you, the more earnings you make. As a matter of fact, compounding makes your money grow exponentially.

For compounding to work it requires two items. The first is **time**. The longer you have to invest, or the younger you are, the more time you have for compounding to do its job. The second component of compounding is the **reinvestment of earnings**. This means that if you invest the earnings you made from your investments, you will generate additional money on those earnings. The alternative would be to take your earnings and spend it. Let's take a look at an example:

Let's say you invest $5,000 today at a 3% interest rate compounded annually. After one year you will have $5,150 (See Table 1.1). Therefore, we made $150 in interest in the first year. Now, let's say that rather than withdraw the $150 you gained from interest, you keep it in there for another year. If you continue to earn the same rate of 3%, your investment will grow to about $5,305 (See Table 1.1). Because you reinvested the $150 you earned in the first year, it works together with your original $5,000 investment, earning you $154.50 the next year, which is $4.50 more than the previous year. Looking ahead to year five, our interest earned in that year is $168.83. Now that may not seem like a lot of money to you and you might be asking yourself, "Who cares about an additional $18.83 in interest when compared to year one?" However, if you keep your money in there and do not take it out for any reason, over a long period of time that $18.83 more that you made in the second year will become hundreds, if not thousands, of dollars more in subsequent years. By comparison, if you decide to withdraw your $150 in interest every year, you will never make additional money on your earnings. In other words, your money will never take advantage of compounding and you will always earn just $150 each year.

Table 1.1

COMPOUND INTEREST				
Year	Money Invested	Interest Rate	Interest Received	Total Amount
1	$5,000	3.00%	$150.00	$5,150
2	$5,150	3.00%	$154.50	$5,305
3	$5,305	3.00%	$159.14	$5,464
4	$5,464	3.00%	$163.91	$5,628
5	$5,628	3.00%	$168.83	$5,796

One thing to keep in mind is that interest rates change on a daily basis. As of this writing, interest rates are at historic lows. Therefore, to find any bank paying 3% interest on your savings is very difficult. However, compounding applies to the stock market as well, along with other types of investments. Historically speaking, the stock market has returned an average of around 10% per year. Therefore, although 3% interest seems very difficult to make in a savings account right now, it is reasonable, although certainly not guaranteed, to expect a return of 3% or more per year in the stock market over a long period of time.

THE INVESTING PROCESS

Investing is not gambling. Investing is a planned process by which you establish short-term and long-term goals and implement the plan to meet or exceed your goals. It is a process by which you attain your goals with the least amount of risk possible by choosing an appropriate variety of investments. Below is a list of important steps in the process of investing that we will be discussing throughout the book:

1. Build emergency savings as a reserve
2. Prepare a budget
3. Establish short and long-term goals
4. Create a plan
5. Implement the plan
6. Monitor and review the plan periodically
7. Make appropriate changes

Notice how the first step in becoming wealthy is to build a reserve for unexpected emergencies. Being young once, I realize now that it appeared unlikely that anything bad would ever happen to me and that I was somewhat immune and invincible to the hardships of life. However, we do get older; trust me, and there are many events that will happen in your life, positive and negative, that will significantly affect your financial future. That is why you should build a cash reserve. The rule of thumb is to put away 3-6 months of your annual income into an emergency fund, usually in a savings account at a bank. As a teenager you may not have a large amount of income or maybe you do not have *any* income right now. However, it is still a smart idea to set aside some of your money in case the unexpected rears its ugly head early in your life.

HOW TO ACCUMULATE MONEY TO INVEST

Most teenagers do not have $5,000 to invest, but there are many ways to accumulate money to start investing. Many teenagers receive money as gifts. Rather than spend the gift money, you could save or invest it. Furthermore, it is important to note that you can invest with as little as $25 per month in some cases.

Let's talk about some other ways to find money to invest. One obvious way is to go out and get a job even if it is only for the summer. It is not difficult to make $2,000, $3,000, or even $4,000 over one summer. It could be something as simple as babysitting, mowing lawns, shoveling driveways, or doing chores around your house for an allowance.

At a young age it is very difficult to imagine yourself far into the future. It is much easier (and more fun) to take your money and buy items such as video games, cell phones and nice cars. As an Investment Management and Wealth Management teacher, I have seen many students walk into my classroom with smart phones. Now I am certainly not saying you shouldn't go out and buy a smart phone, and I'm certainly not saying that having a smart phone as a teenager or young adult is a waste of money. However, over the years we have become a society of wanting things, and wanting them now. We have also become a society of wanting better things than our friends. Think about it. There have been many times when I have heard students talking about waiting in line all night at Best Buy for the latest new video game to come out. There is nothing wrong with wanting to buy a new video game. However, if your first priority is to wait in line all night for the latest and greatest video game to come out so you can be the first one to have it, you should really take a long, hard look at what is most important in your life. Personally, most products I buy are not the latest and greatest model. Most of the time, I will buy last year's model, saving money that I could use to invest. Most brand new models are not much different than the previous year's model. However, you wind up paying much more for the latest and greatest edition.

This all comes down to discipline. There is nothing wrong with wanting things and buying things for yourself. There is nothing wrong with going on vacation. There is nothing wrong with buying a car. We all have our wants and needs. However, like anything else, there needs to be a balance. And as far as having a better cell phone or video game than your friends, we need to take a step back and learn to recognize the important things in life. Think about it this way. If you have balance and discipline in your life when it comes to money, you will be so far ahead of the game financially than your peers. While many of your friends may be in debt and living paycheck to paycheck, you can live a relatively stress-free life.

Something else that amuses me is when students walk in my classroom with a Starbucks coffee or an overpriced energy drink. Many of these drinks cost anywhere between one dollar and three dollars and sometimes more. Not only are these drinks unhealthy for you, they cause you to spend a great deal of money each week or even each month on these items. Let's say that you buy one of these drinks three times a week. And let's say it costs you six dollars a week. There are 4.3 weeks in a month. Multiply $6 times 4.3, and you get around $26. $26 a month may not seem like a lot of money. But imagine using the $26 per month to begin investing. Although you will not accumulate thousands of dollars right away, you are well on your way to becoming wealthy. Remember, one of the major components of compounding is time. Investing just $26 a month when you are young will reap great rewards in your financial future.

Think about some of the things you do and products you buy on a daily or weekly basis. It could be very simple things, like a giant-sized candy bar at the local convenience store or a burger and super-sized drink at a fast food restaurant. Again, it could be products like your cell phone, if you pay for your own cell phone, or a smart phone. You could always call your service provider and maybe switch to a discounted plan. And speaking of a smart phone, you should ask yourself if you really need one. Most smart phones require you to sign up for a data plan. Data plans usually cost about $30 per month. Right there, you could take that $30 a month and start investing for your future. The point I am making is that there are many ways to find money to invest.

STOCKS, BONDS, MUTUAL FUNDS, & CASH INVESTMENTS

Now that we have talked about how to find money to invest, let's talk about some of the major investments that are available to us. In this next section we will be discussing the basics of stocks, bonds, mutual funds, and even cash investments. We will discuss these investments in detail in later chapters.

So what exactly is a stock, and why do we invest in stocks? The most basic answer is that we invest in stocks to make money. When investing in stocks, you are actually part owner of the company. That's right! For example, even if you own only one share of McDonald's stock you are actually part owner of that company. It is a very small slice of McDonald's; a very tiny piece. However, you are an owner of the company. Let's assume McDonald's stock cost $60 per share. If you buy one share of McDonald's stock for $60, and the stock goes up to $80 over the next year, you've made $20 on that investment (See Table 1.2).

Table 1.2

Buy Price	Current Price	Profit
$60	$80	$20

However, McDonald's also pays what is called a *dividend.* Simply put, a dividend is the profit that a company earns and shares with the owners. Imagine that! Simply for owning stock in McDonald's, you will receive profit from the company for doing absolutely nothing. Now, let's say you buy 100 shares of McDonald's. Let's also assume that McDonald's pays a $2 dividend per share every year. That means that every year you will receive $200 in dividends from McDonald's. What should we do with that $200? If you said reinvest the dividends, you are absolutely correct! Take the $200, and reinvest those dividends into more shares of McDonald's stock. As we learned in the previous section, this is a form of compounding. As long as we own McDonald's stock, and as long as we keep reinvesting the dividends, our investment will continue to compound over the years. And over the years you will see that not only would you have your original investment in 100 shares of McDonald's, you would accumulate potentially hundreds more shares of the stock because you were reinvesting the dividends. The whole idea is not to touch your investment. And that is the hard part for teenagers as well as adults. It is very easy to sell your stocks so you can buy something that you want, such as the latest and greatest video game or an expensive pair of sneakers. That is also where discipline comes in. Unless it is an absolute emergency, you should keep your stocks and let them compound over the years. This does not mean that you cannot buy anything you desire. Remember that you need balance in your life, including your finances. We are not saying never to go on vacation or never spend money on entertainment. We are saying that you should PAY YOURSELF FIRST by putting money away for long-term investing. Better yet have a plan. Promise yourself that you will put aside and invest a certain amount of money every month. Stick to your promise. Anything you have left can certainly be invested or spent on yourself.

In general, the stock market has gone up an average 10% a year historically. A 10% return per year seems very good. However, this does not come without risk. One of the terms relating to stocks I would like to discuss is *volatility*. Stocks tend to be volatile. In other words, stocks tend to rise and fall more dramatically than other investments. This does not mean you should never invest in stocks. It simply means you should understand there are no guarantees. There are no guarantees on any investment. However, since you are young, you can afford to take on more risk.

Now let's take a look at bonds. Bonds are the polar opposite of stocks. When we invest in bonds, we become a lender, also known as a creditor. We are not owners of a company. When we invest in bonds, we lend a certain amount of money to a company or government. In return we receive interest payments over a period of time. Let's assume the bonds paid interest for 10 years. We would receive interest every six months for the next 10 years, as long as we own the bonds. After 10 years, we receive our original investment back. For example, if we invest $10,000 in a bond from IBM at a 6% interest rate over 10 years, we would receive $600 of interest per year (or $300 every six months) for 10 years. Over the 10 years, that would be $6,000 in interest received. We would then get the $10,000 back, which was our original investment (See Table 1.3).

Table 1.3

$10,000 in a 10-Year Bond at 6%			
Year	Interest Rate	Interest Received	Total Interest
1	6.00%	$600	$600
2	6.00%	$600	$1,200
3	6.00%	$600	$1,800
4	6.00%	$600	$2,400
5	6.00%	$600	$3,000
6	6.00%	$600	$3,600
7	6.00%	$600	$4,200
8	6.00%	$600	$4,800
9	6.00%	$600	$5,400
10	6.00%	$600	**$6,000**

While stocks tend to be more volatile, bonds tend to be more stable. Therefore, bonds tend to be less risky. This is not to say that bonds cannot be risky. It simply means that in general, bonds are less risky investments.

Another major investment that you will most likely invest in is a mutual fund. A mutual fund is a collection of stocks and/or bonds and possibly cash. One of the major advantages of a mutual fund is that they are well diversified. *Diversification* is an important way to manage risk in your investment portfolio. We will talk in detail about diversification in the next chapter, but in short, it simply means that you have a variety of investments in your portfolio to manage your risk. For example, if you invested $5,000 in just one stock, and that stock went way down for whatever reason, you could, or would, lose much of your money. Conversely, if the stock goes up, you could make a lot of money. Now let's change the situation. Instead of buying $5,000 in one stock, you invest in a mutual fund that consists of 100 stocks. One of the stocks goes down close to zero. Not good, of course, but how will that impact your original investment? Most likely, very little. You still have 99 other stocks to help manage the risk of the one stock. Conversely, if one stock within the mutual fund went up, let's say, 500%, your gain would be tempered by the other 99 stocks.

The last major investment is cash. You may not consider cash as an investment, but that is not completely true. Cash investments can simply be your savings or checking account, money market account, or certificate of deposits (CDs). CDs, in particular, are intriguing cash investments. If you have money in your bank account that you do not need any time soon, it makes sense to purchase a CD from your bank. Although the interest is certainly not great in our current economic environment, it will be significantly more than the interest you receive in your savings account. Furthermore, it is as simple as walking into your bank and requesting a CD. The whole process may take about 15 minutes of your time. There you go....you have already learned how to maximize your investment returns!

These cash investments do not pay much in interest as you may know. However, your risk is greatly limited. There is virtually no risk with these investments which is why your reward is limited. Remember, higher risk, higher POTENTIAL reward. Lower risk, lower reward.

PREPARING A BUDGET

Before we can even consider investing, we need to discuss the importance of a *budget*. If we do not know where our money is going, we will not have any money to invest. That's where a budget becomes relevant to investing. Budgeting is an easy technique where you estimate your income and expenses. By doing this, you can monitor how much money you are spending on certain items and services. Basically, what we are saying is you need to know where your money is going. You need to know how much money is coming in and how much money is going out. This is also called *cash flow*. If more money is going out than coming in, you have negative cash flow. If more money is coming in than going out, you have positive cash flow. Only if we have positive cash flow can we begin investing our money.

Another advantage of a budget is to determine where you can cut costs. For example, you may have $500 per month towards spending and entertainment costs. However, you realize that you could probably reduce that to $400 per month after realizing that you do not spend $500 per month towards spending and entertainment. Now you just found an additional $100 per month to invest!

Most teenagers will not have or need $500 per month or even $400 per month to use towards spending and entertainment costs. However, the above example also pertains to adults. Just imagine if you were an adult and you did not maintain a budget. This means that in any given month you have no idea how much you are spending on expenses. This simple example is a typical scenario for many grown-ups. As a teacher and independent financial adviser, it never ceases to amaze me how many adults have no idea where their money is going. This is how many adults get into financial trouble. A good friend of mine has a well-paying job and easily makes over $100,000 per year. However, he and his wife do not maintain a budget. As a matter of fact, they have never even sat down and talked about where their money goes. You would think that someone who makes that kind of money year after year would be rather wealthy. However, they have what we call negative net worth. Net worth is simply how much cash you would have after selling all of your assets (things you own), and paying off all of your liabilities, (money that you owe). At their ages, they should have somewhere between $400,000 and $600,000 in net worth. Because they do not have a budget, they have no idea how much money they spend each month. They also have maxed out their credit cards, not only once, but twice. After maxing out their credit cards the first time, they depleted their retirement accounts and paid off the credit cards. Sure enough, they maxed out their credit cards again.

Table 1.4

Personal Monthly Budget	
TOTAL MONTHLY TAXABLE INCOME:	
SAVINGS GOALS	
Savings Goal #1	
Savings Goal #2	
Savings Goal #3	
Savings Goal #4	
TOTAL SAVINGS GOALS	
TAXES	
Federal Income Taxes	
State Income Taxes	
Social Security Taxes	
Medicare Taxes	
TOTAL TAXES	
HOUSING/UTILITIES	
Rent	
Insurance	
Electricity, Gas	
Cable TV	
House Phone	
Cell Phone	
Water, Sewage, Garbage	
Other	
TOTAL HOUSING/UTILITIES	
FOOD	
Groceries	
Fast food	
Dining Out	
Other	
TOTAL FOOD	

PERSONAL	
Clothing/Shoes/Hats/Ties/Etc.	
Personal Care (cosmetics/toiletries)	
Laundry Supplies	
Birthday Gifts	
Christmas Gifts	
Hair Cuts	
Other	
TOTAL PERSONAL	
TRANSPORTATION	
Auto Insurance	
License and registration fees	
Gas	
Normal car maintenance	
Bus/Train Expenses	
Cabs	
Other	
TOTAL TRANSPORTATION	
HEALTH	
Over-the-Counter Medications	
Contact Lens Items	
Prescription Co-Pays	
Medical Co-Pays	
Dental Expenses	
Health Club	
Vision	
Other	
TOTAL HEALTH	
ENTERTAINMENT	
Movies	
Concerts	
Sports events	
Video Rental	
Vacation/Trips	
Parties	
Magazine Subscriptions	
Hobbies	
Electronic equipment (software, CDs)	
Sports/Recreation equipment	
Other	
TOTAL ENTERTAINMENT	
LOAN PAYMENTS	
Car Loan	
Student Loan	
Other	
TOTAL LOAN PAYMENTS	
MISCELLANEOUS	
Miscellaneous Items/Expenses	
TOTAL MONTHLY EXPENSES	
TOTAL SURPLUS/DEFICIT	

My friend is a perfect example of how many people in our country live their lives. They live paycheck to paycheck, not knowing where any of their money goes and wondering why they have nothing to show for it. This is why a budget is so important. I certainly realize that most teens do not have many expenses right now. However, it is important to get into the habit of knowing how much money you have coming in and how much money you have going out. This is not a difficult task. It is a smart idea for you to write down all of your expenses you have right now. Also write down how much money you have coming in from a job or even money from chores or gifts. Use the example in table 1.4 below to help you organize your finances. (Note: I have included many expenses that you may not have right now in table 1.4 because I want you to account for them in the future). There are also many useful budget spreadsheets you can find online and download for your benefit. If you get into the habit of maintaining a budget you will understand the importance of knowing where your money goes and, therefore, be way ahead of the game when you graduate college and begin your first significant job.

I would like to mention one more thing on budgeting. I just want you to realize how many actual expenses you will have in the near future. Understand that you will be paying for things such as a mortgage on your house, property taxes, food, utilities, transportation, insurance, entertainment, vacation, and much more. To give you an idea of how all these expenses add up, I give you a realistic example of expenses you may incur for a typical family of four. Let's take a look at table 1.5.

Table 1.5

EXPENSES	MONTHLY
Mortgage	$2,000
Clothing	$150
Dental	$25
Eyecare	$110
Co-Pays/Prescriptions	$30
Haircut	$60
Groceries	$1,000
Gifts	$200
Health/Dental Insurance	$150
Auto Insurance	$100
Home Insurance	$75
Life Insurance	$88
Dry Cleaning	$20
Books/Magazines	$10
Gym Fees	$50
Monthly Spending	$500
School Lunches	$90
Parties/Events	$100
Household Products	$100
Pet Expenses	$75
Driveway	$0
Household Items	$100
Landscaping	$60
Pool Club	$35
Household Repairs	$100
School Expenses	$25
Sports Fees	$125
Musical Lessons	$85
Cable	$120
Electricity	$300
Internet	$0
Newspaper	$12
Sewer	$26
Telephone	$170
Garbage	$35
Water	$80
Lodging	$100
Airfare	$100
Vacation Money	$150
EZPass	$10
Gasoline	$225
Maintenance/Repairs	$100
Registration/Inspection	$25
Bank Charges	$3
Donations	$25
Miscellaneous	$100
Property Taxes	$0
Car Payment	$0
TOTAL MONTHLY	**$7,044**
TOTAL YEARLY	**$84,522**

Notice the total expenses that you will be paying over the course of a year-$84,522! Keep in mind that you will be paying for these expenses from your take-home pay. Net pay is another word for take-home pay. Your net pay is the amount of money you have left **AFTER** all deductions are taken out of your paycheck. $84,522 may seem like a lot of money to you, but keep in mind that your household will likely consist of yourself, your spouse, and children. There are many households I have encountered that have much more than $84,522 a year in expenses. There are also households that have much less than $84,522 in expenses. With this in mind, you need to realize that just because somebody has more in expenses or less in expenses does not mean that they can be labeled as wealthy or not wealthy. Everyone has their own unique situation. The trick is to maintain a healthy and happy lifestyle and live within your means.

Recall that you should pay yourself first. In other words, the first thing you should do with the money you earn is to put away money for saving and investing. Whatever is left should be used for your expenses. If you find you do not have enough to cover your expenses, there are two things you can do: get an additional job or reduce your expenses. While getting an additional job is certainly an option, reducing your expenses would be the easier route to go. The only time you should pay your expenses first is if you have any additional loans to pay off, such as a credit card bill. Aside from that situation, never pay your expenses without paying yourself first!

If you want to look into budgeting in more detail, there are many websites out there that can help you practice, such as budgettracker.com and others. There are also tools you can use such as spreadsheets to develop a budget. You can find many budget spreadsheets already created from companies like Microsoft and Google. There are also many software programs that you can use to create and maintain a budget. A good example of this would be Quicken. Some of these software programs are challenging to learn, but are well worth your time.

"Investing is the most essential topic that a young person needs to know about. However, it is also the topic that so many young people do not fully understand."

-Michael Cramer, Duquesne University

CHAPTER TWO

THE FRUGAL INVESTOR

One sunny day after school you and your best friend decide to take a ride over to Best Buy to check out the latest and greatest smart phone that just came out. You spend a few minutes playing with the new technology and incredible applications the phone already has installed on it. Overcome by the amazing screen display and all of the marketing gimmicks surrounding the phone, you decide that you really want to buy it because you just "have to have it." Eager to make the purchase, you race to your bank while hoping you will not be pulled over for a speeding ticket. Thankfully you arrive just in time because the bank was closing in ten minutes. After withdrawing half of your savings to pay for the expensive smart phone, you hurry back to Best Buy and make the purchase while signing up for a 2-year contract that you cannot terminate without being charged a hefty cancellation fee. But that's okay because now you have a better phone than most of your peers. Besides, you convince yourself that this is the last time you are going to buy a product that is really expensive. In your mind, the smart phone is all you needed.

Meanwhile, your best friend is in awe of your new phone, but refrained from buying one impulsively. Her disappointment does not last long, however, as she is proud of herself for not spending much of her savings on this one item. She decides to keep her relatively new, fully functional, not so glamorous phone and invest some of her money that she has saved up.

A few years later, after graduating college, you land your first significant job and are excited about the beginning of your career and living in your own apartment. Although you have a dependable car that is a little over five years old, you start thinking about buying a new car because you are now making enough money from your new job to make the loan payments. "Who cares about saving and investing my money right now", you say to yourself convincingly. "I am still young so I have plenty of time to worry about retirement. Right now I *need* a new car."

That weekend you visit your local Lexus dealer and are captivated by the shiny, technologically-advanced new cars in the showroom. You test drive one of the models that has all of the upgrades including a sunroof, Blu-Ray player, premium sound system, and the best navigation system money can buy. The salesman seems very knowledgeable and understands your *need* for a new car. He is so interested in getting to know you that you feel he may become a new friend. You may even wind up hanging out with him drinking tea, eating expensive cookies, and telling funny college stories. He tells you that there is a special deal on the car today, and only today, and that he can provide you with a loan as well as a great deal on an extended warranty. Overwhelmed by the new car smell and the genuine feeling that this guy really cares about fulfilling your *needs*, you sign the paperwork and drive off with your new depreciating asset, a $499 per month car loan payment, and much higher auto insurance premiums. But that's okay because your paycheck will cover these costs each month and you just "have to have it". Besides, you convince yourself that you have everything you need and now you can think about saving and investing for your future.

Meanwhile, your best friend also begins her career and a life on her own. She is stunned by your new car and congratulates you on your fine purchase. However, she decides to 'upgrade' from her ten year old car to a five year old car. She is comfortable with this decision because she knows she can save some money on repairs and gas with the newer car. However, she also understands she will not have a hefty car payment to make each month. As a matter of fact, she might not have a car payment at all because she had money saved up for a big purchase. Although her 'new' car is certainly not as alluring as yours, it has all of the basic features most drivers would want including power steering, power locks and windows, and a decent sound system. She knows she can continue to invest some of her paycheck into a retirement plan through her employer. Additionally, she still has money she can use to purchase additional investments that she can use for short-term and long-term financial goals.

Your life has dramatically changed over the past ten years. Married, with two young children, you realize you are going to need to move out of your efficient, but undersized apartment and into a single family home. While searching for a home for your family is adding stress to your life, you find it enjoyable to explore what might become your biggest purchase yet. Many of the homes you and your spouse visit are quite charming and are located in clean, safe areas in quality school districts. These homes are not too big, not too small, and have decent sized yards where your kids can play. But then your realtor brings you to a development that looks like a mini paradise. Massive homes line the streets and provide a background for the championship golf course, Olympic size pool, and luxurious clubhouse. As you stare in awe at the many amenities seemingly persuading you to buy into a piece of the 'good life', you notice many high-priced sports cars passing by. "This is *the* place to be!" you think out loud. "Why can't I be a part of this exclusive development?" you justifiably ask yourself. Three months later you and your family move into your ridiculously oversized house and begin making hefty mortgage payments while paying astronomical utilities expenses for heating and cooling your large dwelling, also referred to by some people as a 'McMansion'. You also had to fill up all the space in your high-priced, glorified money pit by purchasing all kinds of furniture using credit you received from the stores. But that's okay because they do not require that you make any payments for two years! After two years they will charge you an enormous interest rate and you will owe them much more than what you actually paid for the furniture. You rationalize this by thinking you will earn a hefty raise from your employer so you will be able to afford the additional interest you will be charged in a couple of years. This is all okay with you because now you can enjoy golf any time you want as long as you pay your monthly maintenance fees for the 'privilege' of living in such a posh neighborhood. Of course you may have to find a part-time job to help pay for all of these 'necessary' expenses. You are comfortable with your decision though because your friends and family will admire your new lifestyle and look at you in a different, yet not necessarily envious, way. Besides, you just had to have this house. As far as saving and investing for your future, you subconsciously block it out of your mind for the time being because you become too stressed out thinking about it. You tell yourself you will worry about that when the time comes.

Your best friend also bought a house recently. Her home is located on the other side of town, but only a few miles from your neighborhood. She and her husband bought a modest home that has four bedrooms, two and a half bathrooms, an updated kitchen, living room, and a spacious playroom for her two children. Her mortgage payment is well within their budget and she has plenty of money left over to save and invest for retirement, college expenses for her children, and other big-ticket items that she may want or need in the future.

The scenario above is not meant to dissuade you from having a decent smart phone, car, house, or other expensive items, but is intended to make you think before you act impulsively when making large purchases. There is nothing wrong with having nice things, going on vacations, and spending money on products that are unnecessary, but gratifying. However, it is important to maintain a balance in your life, including your finances. If you find that you do not have enough money to cover your expenses, you are probably living above your means. You will need to review your lifestyle and lower or alleviate costs related to frivolous items that are beginning to control your financial well-being. To summarize, you need to live at or below your means.

AN ALL TOO COMMON STORY

A colleague of mine is a new teacher at my school and is 26 years old. She is very bright, hard-working, and will have a fulfilling career as a high school teacher. For the purpose of this case study we'll call her Miss Rationalization (For your information, she gave me permission to use her situation for this book!). Miss Rationalization had a really cool sports car when she was first hired. Not long into her first year teaching, her car started to incur huge costs due to several big issues with the engine and various electronic components. It was quite clear to Miss Rationalization that she needed to buy a newer car rather than dump a few thousand dollars into the one she owned. Given these facts, it was difficult to argue otherwise. However, there is more to this story. Miss Rationalization had some hefty loans for college that were hovering over her like hungry hyenas circling their prey. It would be foolish for her to begin saving and investing until the loans were fully paid off. So now she was faced with a double-edged sword, having a need for a newer car while trying to pay off her student loans. In your opinion, how do you think Miss Rationalization should handle this dilemma?

First of all we need to acknowledge that she definitely needs to purchase a newer car. It does not make sense to spend thousands of dollars on repairing a car that seems to be 'stealing' money from her every time she tries to make a student loan payment. The smart thing for her to do would be to buy a dependable used car that is in good mechanical shape and has relatively low mileage. A car like this might not be the most exciting car to drive, but Miss Rationalization is not in a position to buy one just because it looks good. There are many used cars that fit the description above. It may take a little research and patience, but it would be well worth her time. Because she would be making the financially intelligent choice by being frugal with her money rather than waste it on another "cool" car, Miss Rationalization would have more money to pay off her student loans sooner. Paying off her loans sooner would allow her to begin to invest her money at a younger age, leading to greater wealth and prosperity.

By now you probably have figured out that Miss Rationalization did not make the right *financial* decision. Instead, Miss Rationalization bought a brand new Nissan Sentra Sport Edition equipped with all the bells and whistles including an expensive navigation system, sunroof, satellite radio, iPod docking station, spoiler, and premium exterior detailing. Yes, she was excited to drive this depreciating asset off the car lot after signing her life away. When reality hit though, she suddenly was in much more debt than expected and came to the realization that it will be a very long time when she can actually make her money work for her and not for the banks that provided her the loans.

These are the types of financial decisions that all young people will eventually have to make throughout their lifetimes. Hopefully, you will remember this book and take a step back before buying products and services impulsively. For example, when you are on your way to school in the morning, do you really need to buy that expensive energy drink? Do you really need to buy the latest Xbox game that just came out that day? And how about your prom dress? Is it truly necessary to purchase one that is severely overpriced? I am willing to bet that you can find a dress that is similar to the expensive one, yet fairly priced.

At the risk of repeating myself, I feel the need to stress having balance in your life. Having balance is vital to your overall happiness and sanity throughout your lifetime. This includes balance with your finances, family and friends, career, and religious beliefs. Making important decisions will affect balance in your life. One of the most important decisions I made was related to my career. For four years as a financial advisor at Merrill Lynch, I was working long hours to develop a solid client base. While I enjoyed what I was doing and was reasonably successful, my family life was suffering. At the time, I had a five year old son as well as a newborn son. It was difficult not being able to see my children as much as I wanted.

While still at Merrill Lynch I discovered an opportunity to return to a teaching career as an educator of financial education at a local high school through my network of friends and business contacts. After being offered the teaching position, I had a decision to make that significantly affected my career. If I stayed at Merrill Lynch, I would certainly have a rewarding and lucrative career, but my family life would suffer. If I accepted the teaching position, I would have more time to spend with my family, but I would take a considerable pay cut. Ultimately, I decided to return to teaching, especially since it meant teaching financial education classes. When I look back at the choice I made I have no regrets. I have had time to enjoy watching my sons grow up while enjoying a satisfying career educating teenagers about personal finance and investing. Leaving the long hours at Merrill Lynch has allowed me to have enough time to have a good balance in my life. This is not to say that a career at Merrill Lynch or any other company is not a good choice. The fact of the matter is that everyone needs to put the time in at their job to be successful in their career. Everyone has their own unique situation. The best choice for me at that time was to change careers. Your situation may be much different and require you to take your personal goals and issues into consideration when making important decisions. Hopefully you will make good choices that will provide balance in your life.

"Frivolous spending is the demise of any teenager or young adult. It is imperative to differentiate between wants and needs in order to spare yourself from financial hardship"

-Arianna Miskel, Fordham University

CHAPTER THREE

BASIC CONCEPTS OF INVESTING

You are 18 years old. You just finished reading 'The Early Investor'. You try to contain your excitement. You would like to open an investment account now and start investing and growing your money. As a former teenager, I completely understand how excited you must be. You just learned that it is not rocket science to become wealthy. It just requires financial discipline.

In this chapter, we will discuss some basic financial concepts that you need to know prior to investing your money. This will enable you to form a solid foundation and platform to begin your journey to financial independence. Although some of the topics here might seem dull, it is vital that you learn these basic concepts to control risk in your investment portfolio.

Ask yourself this question: how much of my money should I invest in stocks? More specifically, what percentage of my money should be invested stocks? The answer is not as black and white as it may seem. It depends on many variables such as your age, risk tolerance, and your financial goals. However, we can use a general rule as a starting point. Simply take 100% and subtract your age. Assuming you are 18 years old, 82% of your money should be invested in stocks. Having 82% of your money in stocks may seem very risky. And certainly, to some degree, it can be risky. Keep in mind though that this is simply a starting point. There are questions you need to ask yourself about how you are going to use the money that you accumulate. Questions such as:

- Will I need this money within the next 3 to 5 years?
- Is the money I am investing going to be used for my future retirement?
- How comfortable am I with the volatility in the stock market?

After understanding your short-term and long-term goals as well as your risk tolerance, you are ready to create an appropriate *asset allocation* for your investment portfolio. What exactly is asset allocation? Asset allocation is a strategy that divides your assets among major types of investments such as stocks, bonds, real estate, and cash in order to balance risk and create diversification. For example, if you have $20,000 to invest and your asset allocation is 50% stocks, 25% bonds, 20% in real estate investments and 5% in cash, you would be investing $10,000 in stocks, $5,000 in bonds, $4,000 in real estate investments, and $1,000 in cash investments.

One of the major reasons that we use asset allocation as a risk management technique is due to fluctuations in the stock market. Imagine for a moment that you have 100% of your money invested in stocks. The stock market goes down close to 50% that year. Using the $20,000 you had to invest from above, you could lose approximately $10,000 in that one year (See Table 3-1).

Table 3.1

Total Investments	% of Investments in Stocks	% of Investments in Bonds	Market Decline	Ending Portfolio Value
$20,000	100.00%	0.00%	50.00%	**$10,000**

And yes, there have certainly been years when the stock market has gone down close to 50% in one year. Now let's say we have 60% of our money in stocks and 40% in bonds and once again, the stock market goes down close to 50% in that year. However, the bond market goes up around 20% in the same year. Understand that typically when stocks prices go down, bond prices go up. This is certainly not always true, but it is rare when both stocks and bonds go up together or down together. Let's see what happens now. Using the asset allocation of 60% in stocks and 40% in bonds, we can see from Table 3-2 below that our stock portion was worth approximately $12,000 in the beginning and could now be worth approximately $6,000 due to the stock market going down. However, because we had 40% of our money in bonds and the bond market went up 20% that year, our bond portion of our portfolio is worth $9,600. The $9,600 was calculated by taking 40% of the original 20,000, which comes out to $8,000, and multiplying that by 1.2, which is 120%. You could also multiply the $8,000 times 20%, which is a $1,600 gain, and add that back to the $8,000. In total, at the end of this year, our investment portfolio is worth $15,600. This is not exactly something to be happy about. However, if we had 100% of our money in stocks, our investment portfolio would be worth only $10,000 after that year.

Table 3.2

Total Stock Investments	Total Bond Investments	Stock Market Decline	Bond Market Return	Ending Portfolio Value
$12,000	$8,000	50.00%	20.00%	$15,600*

**This value is computed by adding the ending values of your stocks and bonds ($6,000 in stocks & $9,600 in bonds)*

There is one important concept you should understand related to the above scenarios. As shown above, if we begin with $20,000 invested in stocks and the stock market goes down 50% that year, we could be left with approximately $10,000 at the end of the year. Some people might suggest that our stocks would have to go up 50% from this point to get back to our original $20,000. This is definitely not the case. If our $20,000 investment portfolio went down 50% to $10,000, and the stock market went up 50% the following year, our portfolio would only be worth $15,000, which is still $5,000 less than the original $20,000 we began with (See Table 3.3). It may be obvious to you that the reason is because we began the second year with a lower amount. However, it is nice to see the actual numbers and realize that when you lose money in the stock market, it is not always easy to grow that money back. That is why we must protect our portfolio from too much risk. Asset allocation is the first step in controlling risk in our portfolios.

Table 3.3

Year	Beginning Stock Value	Stock Market Performance	Total Value of Stocks
1	$20,000	Down 50%	$10,000
2	$10,000	Up 50%	$15,000

The next step in controlling risk is called *diversification*. Diversification is another risk management technique that mixes a wide variety of investments within your portfolio. For example, your investments should vary in risk. Within your stock investments, you should not invest in all risky stocks, nor should you invest in all conservative stocks. There is nothing wrong with investing in risky stocks, but if the stock market trends down for an extended period of time, your entire portfolio will be significantly affected in a negative way. Conversely, if you choose stocks that vary in risk and the market trends down, you will likely lose money, but certainly not as much. Some examples of stocks that are historically more risky are Netflix, XMSirius Satellite Radio, and NPSP Pharmaceuticals. Some examples of stocks that are historically less risky are Procter & Gamble, Johnson & Johnson, and Verizon. Keep in mind that although these and other companies may be more or less risky from a historical perspective, future performance and risk levels are not guaranteed.

You should also vary your investments by industry, minimizing specific risk of certain industries. For example, it is not wise to invest all of your money in technology stocks. It is also not wise to invest all of your money in pharmaceutical companies. If you take a look at technology stocks, you will realize that many technology stocks go up and down based on how stocks like Microsoft and Apple perform. Additionally, you will see that when a large pharmaceutical company such as Pfizer goes up or down, most pharmaceutical companies will follow. This is fantastic when these companies go up, but could be a disaster if they go down, especially if they go down dramatically. Imagine if, for whatever reason, Pfizer's stock price goes down 20%. If your portfolio consists of all pharmaceutical companies, most, if not all, of your stocks may go down as well. Conversely, if Pfizer goes up 20%, most or all of your stocks may go up. On the surface, the previous scenario sounds appealing. However, you are taking additional risk that, in most cases, is unnecessary.

Now is a good time to discuss the ultimate sin word in investing; Greed! "Greed, for lack of a better word, is good" is a famous quote from Michael Douglas in the original Wall Street movie. In the movie, Gordon Gekko (Michael Douglas) preaches that greed is not only good, but "greed is right. Greed works. Greed clarifies, cuts through, and captures, the essence of the evolutionary spirit. Greed, in all of its forms; greed for life, for money, for love, knowledge, has marked the upward surge of mankind". As an experienced investor, I can emphatically say that greed is NOT good! Especially greed for money. In the world of investing, greed can be bad. Greed does not work. Greed does not clarify. It distorts our logic. Greed does not cut through. It crashes into a wall. Greed does not capture the essence of the evolutionary spirit. It damages our character and moral fiber. Greed has not marked the upward surge of mankind. Greed has caused many economies to falter which has resulted in hardships for individuals and families around the world.

There is a story I'd like to tell you that I share with my Investment Management students. It involves someone close to me who I will not specifically name. I'll call him "GG", for Gordon Gekko.

Back in the year 2000, GG met a speculative stockbroker. We'll call him "Mr. Slick". A speculative stockbroker is someone who tries to find small companies that have innovative products that are ready to become main stream. While this is great for capitalism, there are literally thousands upon thousands of smaller companies that invent unique products. Trying to find the one that will be successful is like trying to find a needle in a haystack. Anyway, GG opened up an investment account with Mr. Slick and deposited about $200,000 in his account. What should be surprising to you is the fact that GG only had $200,000 in *total* savings. Although a successful business owner, GG never implemented a retirement plan for him and his family. At age 60, he realized that he needed to finally start investing his money to achieve his retirement goals. In some ways, it is justifiable to be risky and try and grow your money quickly beginning at age 60. However, that is easier said than done.

Here is where the story gets interesting. One day Mr. Slick calls GG and tells him to take all of his money and invest it into one stock. Without telling you what stock it was, I can say that the company's product was unique, affordable, and in demand. However, the company was not making a profit. Furthermore, the company had to borrow millions of dollars for research and to stay in business. This is a typical scenario. There are many companies with fantastic products that need to borrow money to stay in business. Very few of these companies actually become successful from a financial standpoint.

GG gets excited and puts all his money into the stock. One week later, some very positive news comes out regarding the stock. The price of the stock went through the roof. Keep in mind that in early 2000, as well as the late 1990s, there was a major bubble in stock prices. It seemed that with any stock you bought the price would go up regardless of how financially sound the company was at the time.

GG calls his close family member, "Mr. Logical" from Mr. Slick's office and proudly announces he has about $3 million in its investment portfolio! Mr. Logical was very happy for his family member, but tried to put the situation in perspective.

"GG that's fantastic!" Mr. Logical said. "You've won the game. You can now retire. Consider yourself lucky. Good for you. Sell all of it."

The question of course is what do you think GG's reply was? Logically speaking, GG should have sold all of the stock and called it a day. He should be thrilled he was that lucky. It is rare that any stock goes up that much in one day.

GG laughed confidently and replied, "Mr. Slick said the stock price is likely to go up further."

"Okay, GG", Mr. Logical nervously said, "but at least sell half of it."

By now you could imagine what happened to the stock and GG's money. After a few days, the stock started trending down. Again, Mr. Logical spoke to GG and tried to persuade him to sell the stock.

"Mr. Slick said that this is normal and that the stock is simply correcting itself after the huge run-up and it will start trending upward again very soon".

Let's fast-forward and discuss what happened to the stock a few months later. Not only did the stock price fall below what GG bought it at, but he never sold any of it. GG ended up with less than his original $200,000, and therefore, lost money! I don't know which is worse; having $3 million and losing it, or never having it at all.

Stories like this are not uncommon. Scenarios such as the story above can be found at all levels. It doesn't matter if you have $1,000 or $10,000,000.

Greed is good, except when you lose all of your money! Personally, I am also guilty of being too greedy. There have been times where I have made a very good profit in stocks, only to see it dwindle away after becoming too risky. You must realize that when investing in stocks, our emotions get the best of us.

There are many investors out there that consider themselves 'day traders'. Day traders are investors who buy and sell stock on a daily basis to profit on the volatility of stock prices. Most day traders use some type of system that will tell them when to buy or sell a stock. Some use their own system, and some purchase a day trading system. You may have seen advertisements on the Internet that claim that you will profit greatly from the stock market if using their system. You should view these advertisements as too good to be true. There is no magical system or crystal ball that is going to make you become wealthy overnight. You might as well go to a casino and gamble. True investing is coming up with a concrete plan to systematically invest your money over a long period of time and by making sound investment choices that will help you reach your goals. If you have a good foundation and are meeting or exceeding your goals, it is okay to have a little *Vegas money*. Remember, only be very risky with some of your money after you have implemented a plan and are reaching your goals. That way, if you lose all of your Vegas money, you are still on track to become wealthy. Never take your money that has been properly allocated to your financial plan and use it as your Vegas money! By the way, the majority of day traders over time have lost money. They may be successful at first, but they quickly realize that betting on stock prices on a daily basis is a path that will eventually lead to losses.

DOLLAR COST AVERAGING

A simple way to begin your quest for great wealth is to use a technique called *dollar cost averaging*, or DCA. DCA is a process of buying a fixed dollar amount of a particular investment on a regular schedule regardless of the share price. Let's take a look at an example of dollar cost averaging.

Jeff, age 18, invests $200 per month in to his investment account. Each $200 buys shares of ABC mutual fund. For the last four months he purchased $200 worth of ABC at prices of $22, $18, $16, and $19. Let's take a look at what has happened on a monthly basis.

After taking Mr. Zisa's Investment Management class, Jeff is very excited as he buys his first $200 of ABC mutual fund. ABC mutual fund goes down to $18 per share after the first month. Jeff is certainly unhappy with this performance. However, remembering what Mr. Zisa had said, he buys $200 more of ABC mutual fund at the same time the following month. Since the mutual fund went down to $18 per share, Jeff has acquired more shares even though he still invested the same $200. Let's compare the first two months. As shown in Table 3-4, Jeff bought about 9.1 shares of ABC mutual fund in the first month. In the second month, Jeff bought approximately 11 shares of ABC mutual fund, about two more shares than he was able to buy in the first month. Now let's take a look at what happens in the third month.

In the third month ABC mutual fund goes down to $16 per share. Now Jeff is very unhappy and wonders what he was thinking when he listened to Mr. Zisa. He has lost six dollars per share from the first month and an additional two dollars per share from the second month. Once again though, he buys another $200 of ABC mutual fund at the same time the following month. Since the mutual fund went down to $16 per share, Jeff was able to buy about 12.5 shares that month. By now you can see what is happening. Certainly in a perfect world, ABC mutual fund would always go up. However, we now know that the stock market can be volatile, and prices can fluctuate on a daily basis. This is where dollar cost averaging can be very powerful. It takes much of the price risk away when purchasing investments.

Table 3.4

Month	Amount Invested	Price per Share	# of Shares Bought
1	$200	$22	9.09
2	$200	$18	11.11
3	$200	$16	12.5
4	$200	$19	10.53

Analyzing the fourth month, we see that ABC mutual fund finally went up to $19 per share. Jeff is very relieved because he sees that he has made a profit from the shares he bought in the second and third month. In the first month he has still lost $3 per share. However, in the second month, he has gained $1 per share and in the third month he has gained $3 per share. Keep in mind that in the second and third month he bought more shares with his $200 when compared to the first month. It would help to see how much he has made (or lost) on a total level. In order to see this, we first need to find the *weighted average* price that he has paid for ABC mutual fund over the first four months. The term weighted average is an average in which some values count more than others. This would be helpful to us because he purchased a different number of shares each month. To find the weighted average price, we first divide each $200 invested by each monthly stock price to find how many shares he purchased each month (See Table 3-4). We can see that Jeff purchased a total of 43.23 shares of ABC mutual fund over the four months (9.09 + 11.11 + 12.50 + 10.53). Next, we divide the total amount invested by the total number of shares purchased. Looking at table 3-4 we can see that Jeff invested a total of $800. $800 divided by 43.23 total shares purchased is about $18.50. Therefore, Jeff has paid roughly $18.50 for each share of the fund. Since the latest price per share is now $19, he made about $.50 per share on his investment. That may not seem like a sizable gain, but remember it has only been four months. On a total dollar level, Jeff has made about $21.62 in four months (43.23 shares owned times $.50 per share profit).

Using dollar cost averaging, young people can begin investing their money for as little as $25 a month in some cases. Mutual fund companies such as Vanguard and Fidelity are good places to start investing using DCA. These companies allow you to automatically take a specific amount of money out of your savings or checking account on a specific day of the month and invest the money in their mutual funds.

By using the basic investing concepts we have discussed, you can begin building a solid foundation for your financial future. Remember that while risk can certainly turn into greater profit, it is essential to use the techniques discussed to prevent disaster in your portfolio. Greed can manipulate logic and cause you to participate in unnecessary risks in the stock market. Conversely, having an appropriate asset allocation, diversifying your investments, and reinvesting your investment earnings can start and keep you on the road to financial success. As a polite suggestion, it would be in your best interest to finish this book before doing anything with your money. Although you likely know more about investing at this point than many adults, there is much more to learn in the upcoming chapters. I would strongly recommend that you do not start investing until carefully reading these chapters as well as consulting with family members or friends who may be in the financial services industry. When well-educated and prepared, you can confidently begin your quest to become wealthy.

"Asset allocation is essential to any portfolio. After reading this chapter, I understand how to diversify my future investment portfolio."

-Nick Young, High School Student

CHAPTER FOUR

WHY SHOULD I INVEST IN STOCKS?

In the first three chapters, we discussed basic investing concepts and basic investments such as stocks, bonds, mutual funds, and cash. In the next few chapters you will learn about stocks, bonds, and mutual funds in greater detail. It is important to understand the specifics of these types of investments in order to become a more knowledgeable investor. Knowledge is power. Knowledge can help you make money, as well as prevent you from losing it.

What exactly is a stock? Furthermore, why does a company issue stock? Does every company have stock? Let's answer the latter question first. Most companies in the United States and abroad are small businesses. These small businesses may be owned by one person or a partnership of two or more people. The majority of small businesses, therefore, are privately owned. When a company is privately owned, there is no stock associated with it, with a few rare exceptions. Throughout a small company's history, the owner or owners may do very well and make a great deal of profit. However, most of these companies will always be privately owned and will never feel the need to issue stock. What do we mean when we say a company issues stock? To help us comprehend this concept, let's take a look at the following scenario.

Company ABC is a successful small business that produces unique widgets for popular electronics products that are sold across the United States. They have been in business for approximately 2 years. Company ABC is a privately owned business that consists of three owners, Rob, Jack, and Kyle. Because their business has thrived due to the unique nature of their widgets, the owners are finding it extremely difficult to keep up with demand. While this is a great problem to have, Rob, Jack, and Kyle need to make some important decisions about the future of Company ABC. On one hand, they could try to sell their successful business to a larger company that can handle the demand for their product. This could certainly be a profitable solution. In many cases, when a company sells out to a larger company, the larger company will give the owners a lucrative position within the company. Not a bad deal for Rob, Jack, and Kyle.

The above scenario is typical among smaller businesses that have been successful. However, there are other alternatives that would let small business owners like Rob, Jack, and Kyle maintain control of their company, yet profit from expansion. Let's take a look at these alternative solutions.

Rob, Jack, and Kyle decide that rather than sell their company, they would like to expand their operations to keep up with demand for their widgets. Since the owners of Company ABC have decided to expand, they will need to generate money. They could certainly obtain a large loan from a financial institution, assuming they would qualify. While certainly a possibility, it may be difficult to acquire a loan given their company has only been in business for two years. Furthermore, the company would be required to pay back the money and make interest payments along the way. This sounds like a very familiar type of investment we learned about in Chapter 1. That's right--bonds. Conversely, they could take Company ABC from a private company to a public company by issuing stock. Before taking you through the process of issuing stock, we need to understand what it means for a company to become public and why it could be advantageous.

In Chapter 1, we learned that when investing in stocks we are part owner of a company. We are considered shareholders and can have a claim on the company's profits in the form of dividends. We can buy stocks in certain corporations because they are public companies. At some point in time, they converted from a private company to a public company. A popular example I use in my classroom is Google. Google began as a private company started by two individuals. As we all know, Google became a household name and is now used by hundreds of millions of people around the world. Because of Google's success, the owners not surprisingly decided to take their company public in 2004 by issuing stock in order to expand their business and keep up with exponential demand. The process by which a company issues stock begins with what is called an IPO, or an initial public offering. This is considered the first sale of a company's stock. Let's briefly take you through the initial public offering process.

After Google decides to become a public company and issue stock, they need to hire an investment firm, as well as attorneys, to create the legal forms and appropriate documents needed. This process can take anywhere from a few months to a year to complete. During the process, Google and its partners agree upon a fixed price for the initial public offering, as well as the number of shares they will issue. For simplicity's sake, let's assume that Google issued one million shares of stock at a price of $50 per share. I can tell you that these numbers are not accurate when looking at Google's initial public offering. However, we are using the numbers above to make the concept easier to understand. Moving along in the process, Google needs to sell most of the one million shares of their initial stock in what is called the *primary market.* Generally speaking, this means that the one million shares are dispersed among many investment firms and sold to their clients, who are investors like you and I. Keep in mind that these investors likely have a great deal of money in their investment accounts. In reality, it can be difficult to obtain shares of stock through an IPO, especially in the case of Google. It is easy to understand that the demand for Google stock was enormous, given their early success. As a former financial adviser at Merrill Lynch, I can recall many conversations in 2004 with my clients that involved the possibility of buying shares of Google's IPO. Since there are a finite number of shares of an IPO, financial advisors and stockbrokers can only offer a limited number of IPO shares to their clients. When most or all of Google's IPO are sold, a date is set where Google's stock will be traded in the *secondary market.* For example, let's assume Google set a date of September 1, 2004 as the first date their stock could begin trading. At this point in time, all investors can begin buying and selling Google stock. In the primary market, Google stock was sold at a fictitious price of $50 per share. In the secondary market, the price is determined by investors who trade the stock throughout the day. The secondary market is where most investors buy and sell stock.

Now that we have learned the process of how a company becomes public and issues stock, let's revisit Company ABC and see how becoming a public company can be advantageous to its owners. Since Rob, Jack, and Kyle are issuing stock, rather than selling the bonds to raise money, they do not have to pay back the money or make interest payments along the way. Furthermore, the majority of the risk associated with the company will now be on the shareholders. This is because the shareholders will own the majority of the company. If Company ABC begins to lose money and their business begins to fail, the stock price can go down dramatically. In theory, the stock price can go down to zero, which has happened to some public companies in the past. Therefore, shareholders are at the risk of losing some or all of their money. The owners of Company ABC will still own shares of the company's stock and are at risk as well. But because they are no longer the only owners of the company, their risk is limited. Now Company ABC will have plenty of money they received from the initial public offering to expand their operations, hire talented employees, meet the demand for their product, and be highly competitive in an always changing economic environment.

We just looked at some of the advantages of taking a company public and issuing stock. However, there are some disadvantages as well. Because shareholders own the majority of the company, Rob, Jack, and Kyle have given up much of the control of their company. There will now be a board of directors for Company ABC that will oversee major decisions made by management. The board of directors is elected by shareholders; each getting one vote per share. While Rob, Jack, and Kyle will likely have a lucrative position within the company even after taking their company public, their jobs are always at risk of being eliminated or replaced by the board of directors and shareholders.

There are actually two types of stock that a company can issue. The first type is called common stock. Common stock shares of a company are the type that most people buy and sell, or trade. Common stock shares:

- Represent ownership in a company and the right to receive dividends
- Have *variable* dividends that are not guaranteed
- Allow investors to get one vote per share for any major decisions the company makes

What is interesting to note is the second bullet point. Common stock shares pay variable dividends. The word variable means changing, or not fixed. Let's discuss variable dividends in more detail.

To help you understand how variable dividends work, let's look at a real-life scenario. Citigroup is one of the biggest banks in the world and one of the most widely held public companies among investors. Up until the mid-2000s, Citigroup had a stellar track record of earnings and paid a solid dividend that they usually increased on a yearly basis. Then came the financial crisis of 2007-2008. Many banks, including Citigroup, made risky investments that caused them to lose billions of dollars. Citigroup had no choice but to wipe out their dividend completely. Remember, dividends are the profits that the company pays out to their shareholders. Since Citigroup started losing money, they had no profits to pay out. They needed to conserve what little cash they had left to cover their losses. Think about the fact that many older, retired people relied on Citigroup's dividends for income. It is my guess that most retired Citigroup investors never thought the dividends they received would be at risk. I remember a close relative of mine calling me up and telling me he just bought Citigroup stock because the stock price dropped dramatically and the dividend yield was somewhere around 25%. That means at the time he bought the stock, he would generate a staggering 25% return on his investment that year just for owning the stock. Assuming he invested $20,000 in Citigroup stock, he would theoretically receive $5,000 in dividends. I didn't quite know how to tell him that it was highly unlikely that Citigroup would be able to maintain their dividend payments. Inevitably, Citigroup soon announced they would be erasing their dividend indefinitely. Today, as of this writing, Citigroup is paying just a .10% dividend, a far cry from the high dividend they paid for so many years. Conversely, there are some companies that have historically increased their dividends every year for a longer period of time. These are the companies with a long track record of solid earnings, who fill a need in the economy. These are companies that are considered boring. These are companies whose stock prices go up and down, but at a less volatile pace. Many of these companies are in the consumer staples sector of the economy and make products and services in industries such as utilities, energy and food. A relevant example of this type of company is Procter and Gamble (PG). Procter & Gamble makes products such as toothpaste, toiletries, and grooming products. Some of the brand names under Procter and Gamble are Gillette, Duracell, Tide, Bounty, and Pampers. With the risk of being facetious, no matter how bad the economy gets, we will always need toilet paper and toothpaste! This makes Procter and Gamble fairly recession proof when compared to most other industries. While we realize that common stocks pay dividends that are never guaranteed, Procter & Gamble has increased their dividend every year for over 50 years and counting. Procter and Gamble certainly is not the only company that has done this, but they are an ideal example of investing in stocks that pay solid, growing dividends.

The second type of stock that a company can issue is called preferred stock. Preferred stock:

- Does not represent the same degree of ownership in a company
- Does not come with the same voting rights
- Usually guarantees a *fixed* dividend forever

Looking at the third bullet point, you probably notice the word fixed instead of variable. This means that investors buy preferred stock for the sole purpose of generating income. As a matter of fact, preferred stock prices are not nearly as volatile as common stock prices. Preferred stock prices are generally very stable, much like bonds. Preferred stock works much like a bond in other ways. Just like a bond, preferred stock gives you a fixed rate of income. Just like a bond, preferred stock does not represent normal ownership in a company. Consequently, when you receive your investment account statements in the mail, your preferred stock is usually listed under the fixed income investments section. However, the one difference between a bond and preferred stock is the fact that preferred stock pays a dividend forever, or as long as you own it. The most important concept you should understand when considering investing in common stock versus preferred stock is that common stock is needed to grow your investment portfolio while preferred stock is used to generate income.

Since we discussed the differences between variable and fixed dividends, I'd like to go into more detail about how dividends work and how they are paid. Let's take a look at the following example.

If company XYZ is paying a $1.62 dividend per share and you own 400 shares, how much will the company pay you that year just for owning shares? To calculate this amount, we simply take 400 shares and multiply that by

$1.62 per share to get $648. (See Table 4.1) That's right! Just for owning the shares you will receive $648 that year. It is important to note that the $648 is not paid out once per year. Most companies pay out their dividends four times per year, or every quarter. Therefore, in the scenario above, you will receive $162 every quarter for a total of $648. This money is credited to your investment account in the form of cash.

Table 4.1

Number of Shares Owned	Dividend Per Share	Yearly Dividends Received
400	$1.62	$648

If you remember back in chapter 1, we learned the concept of compounding and how it can help you become wealthy. We learned that instead of withdrawing any earnings you make from your savings or investments, you should reinvest those earnings to make more money. This simple concept applies to the above scenario. Rather than take the $648 in cash out of your investment portfolio, the smart thing to do would be to reinvest your dividends into more shares of the corresponding stock. This is a very simple technique to do within your investment portfolio. Almost all dividend paying stocks will allow you to automatically reinvest your dividends into additional shares. The process of setting up automatic dividend reinvesting is essentially as simple as checking off a box that says **'automatic dividend reinvestment'** on your investment account forms. At any time, if you decide to stop reinvesting your dividends into more shares, you can simply update your account form by deselecting the same box. You should understand, however, that in order to build great wealth over time, you should always reinvest your dividends to let compounding do its job. The only time you would stop reinvesting your dividends is for emergencies such as job loss or any unexpected large expense that you need to cover. Of course, you should have an emergency fund already set up so you do not have to pull money from your investments.

Another way to buy dividend paying stocks and automatically reinvest the dividends is to open up a dividend reinvestment plan, also known as DRIPs. These are plans with which individual companies, for a minimal cost, allow investors to purchase stock directly from the company. Most large companies provide dividend reinvestment plans; companies such as McDonald's, Microsoft, General Electric, and Walt Disney. A great benefit of opening up a DRIP through one of these companies is that it is much cheaper to purchase their stock through their DRIP plan because you are not going through a stockbroker, who would charge you a commission. You can find out more about opening up a DRIP through these companies by going to their websites and clicking on **Investor Relations**. There is usually an 800 number that you can call to find out more information and set up an account.

One thing to keep in mind when opening up a dividend reinvestment plan is that it can be relatively risky. This is because you are only investing in one company, meaning you are not properly diversified. There is nothing wrong with starting to invest using this technique. However, make sure that as time goes on and as you make more money, you should invest in a variety of stocks or even a variety of DRIPs.

Analyzing Table 4.2 below reveals the power of dividend reinvestment. Before looking at the results, we should understand some of the variables within the chart. The chart assumes investing $2,000 one time, and one time only. In this case, we are buying 100 shares of a stock at $20 per share. We are also assuming that the stock currently pays a $1.00 dividend per share, giving us $100 in total dividends in year one. Moving over to the last column shows us the actual dividend yield; in this scenario 5%. We arrived at a 5% dividend yield by taking the dividend amount in year one and dividing it by your original investment of $2,000 ($100 divided by $2,000 = .05, or 5%).

Table 4.2

Year	Number of Shares	Price	Dividend	Dividend Amount	Total Stock Value	Actual Dividend Yield
1	100	$20.00	$1.00	$100	$2,000	5.00%
2	105	$21.60	$1.08	$113	$2,260	5.65%
3	109	$23.33	$1.17	$128	$2,554	6.38%
4	115	$25.19	$1.26	$144	$2,886	7.21%
5	**120**	**$27.21**	**$1.36**	**$163**	**$3,261**	**8.15%**
6	125	$29.39	$1.47	$184	$3,685	9.21%
7	131	$31.74	$1.59	$208	$4,164	10.41%
8	137	$34.28	$1.71	$235	$4,705	11.76%
9	144	$37.02	$1.85	$266	$5,317	13.29%
10	**150**	**$39.98**	**$2.00**	**$300**	**$6,008**	**15.02%**
11	157	$43.18	$2.16	$339	$6,789	16.97%
12	165	$46.63	$2.33	$384	$7,672	19.18%
13	172	$50.36	$2.52	$433	$8,669	21.67%
14	180	$54.39	$2.72	$490	$9,796	24.49%
15	**188**	**$58.74**	**$2.94**	**$553**	**$11,070**	**27.67%**
16	197	$63.44	$3.17	$625	$12,509	31.27%
17	206	$68.52	$3.43	$707	$14,135	35.34%
18	216	$74.00	$3.70	$799	$15,972	39.93%
19	226	$79.92	$4.00	$902	$18,049	45.12%
20	**236**	**$86.31**	**$4.32**	**$1,020**	**$20,395**	**50.99%**
21	247	$93.22	$4.66	$1,152	$23,046	57.62%
22	259	$100.68	$5.03	$1,302	$26,042	65.11%
23	271	$108.73	$5.44	$1,471	$29,428	73.57%
24	283	$117.43	$5.87	$1,663	$33,253	83.13%
25	**296**	**$126.82**	**$6.34**	**$1,879**	**$37,576**	**93.94%**
26	310	$136.97	$6.85	$2,123	$42,461	106.15%
27	324	$147.93	$7.40	$2,399	$47,981	119.95%
28	339	$159.76	$7.99	$2,711	$54,219	135.55%
29	355	$172.54	$8.63	$3,063	$61,267	153.17%
30	**372**	**$186.35**	**$9.32**	**$3,462**	**$69,232**	**173.08%**
31	389	$201.25	$10.06	$3,912	$78,232	195.58%
32	407	$217.35	$10.87	$4,420	$88,402	221.00%
33	426	$234.74	$11.74	$4,995	$99,894	249.74%
34	445	$253.52	$12.68	$5,644	$112,880	282.20%
35	**466**	**$273.80**	**$13.69**	**$6,378**	**$127,555**	**318.89%**
36	487	$295.71	$14.79	$7,207	$144,137	360.34%
37	510	$319.36	$15.97	$8,144	$162,875	407.19%
38	534	$344.91	$17.25	$9,202	$184,049	460.12%
39	558	$372.51	$18.63	$10,399	$207,975	519.94%
40	**584**	**$402.31**	**$20.12**	**$11,751**	**$235,012**	**587.53%**

Other assumptions include an average yearly rise in the stock price of 8% and an average yearly rise in the dividend per share of 8%. These assumptions, while not guaranteed, can be found in certain stocks. At the end of each year the dividends are reinvested into additional shares of the stock. Looking at year two, we can see that we now have about 105 shares of the stock due to the fact that we reinvested the $100 in dividends we received in year one. We received the additional five shares by dividing $100 by the price of $21.60, the price of the stock at the beginning of year two. In actuality we only bought 4.63 shares of the stock, but in the chart we rounded to the nearest whole number. Notice in year two our dividends went up 8% to $1.08 per share. Consequently, our total dividend amount for year two is $113 and our total stock value in year two is up to $2,260 (104.63 shares times $21.60 per share). Finally, our actual dividend yield in year two is up to 5.65%. The 5.65% comes from the dividend amount in year two, which is $113, divided by your ORIGINAL investment of $2,000.

Although there does not appear to be major differences in the total stock value and the actual dividend yields, as time goes on you will see the power of dividend reinvesting and compounding in action. Let's move ahead to year five. In year five we now have approximately 120 shares of the stock due to reinvesting the dividends. The stock price has also risen to $27.21, and the dividend amount per share is up to $1.36. Our total stock value has increased to $3,261 and our actual dividend yield has risen since the beginning to 8.15%. To put this in perspective, remember that the stock market has historically gone up an average of about 10% per year. This investment is making 8.15% in year five just on the dividends alone! Also, remember that our original investment was only $2,000 and that we are not investing any additional new money into the stock.

Moving ahead to year 10 adds additional excitement when analyzing the numbers. In year 10 we now own 150 shares of the stock, the stock price has nearly doubled, the dividend amount per share is up to $2.00, our total stock value has more than tripled to $6,008, and our actual dividend yield is up to a staggering 15.02%! And if that does not excite you, take a look at year 20. From our original $2,000 investment we now have $20,395 and are making 51% in dividends that year! Finally, moving on to year 40 shows us we have $235,012 in total stock value and are receiving an unimaginable 587.53% in dividends relative to our original investment of $2,000!

From an historical perspective, the overall stock market has risen, on average, around 10% per year. However, there is never a guarantee that you will make money in the long-run when investing in stocks due to the higher risk associated with them. One alternative would be to keep your cash under your mattress or even in a savings account. In the long run, that would be a recipe for disaster because inflation would significantly outpace the buying power of your money. Therefore, you should ask yourself an important question. Knowing that you can use the power of compounding and dividend reinvesting to your advantage, could you earn $2,000 over one summer so you can begin building wealth? I would hope that the answer would be "absolutely" or "of course I could". Hopefully you are also saying to yourself, "why ***wouldn't*** I do this?" I also think it would not be difficult for most teenagers to earn more than $2,000 over the year, or even over one summer. As a matter of fact, if you could earn $5,000 in one year the numbers would change dramatically. (See Table 4.3) Using our previous assumptions, after 40 years our total stock value would be $587,529! Most teens and young adults would be somewhere in the range of 50 years old to 60 years old after 40 years of this investment. I would also like to reiterate that we only invested $5,000 one time in this scenario. In reality, we will invest much more of our money over our lifetime. Keep in mind that there are no guarantees that you will accumulate this amount of money. The amounts in the tables might be lower or even higher. It all depends on how your investment performs over the time period and if the dividend is consistently increased at a high enough rate.

Table 4.3

Year	Number of Shares	Price	Dividend	Dividend Amount	Total Stock Value	Actual Dividend Yield
1	250	$20.00	$1.00	$250	$5,000	5.00%
2	262	$21.60	$1.08	$283	$5,650	5.65%
3	274	$23.33	$1.17	$319	$6,385	6.38%
4	286	$25.19	$1.26	$361	$7,214	7.21%
5	**300**	**$27.21**	**$1.36**	**$408**	**$8,152**	**8.15%**
6	313	$29.39	$1.47	$461	$9,212	9.21%
7	328	$31.74	$1.59	$520	$10,410	10.41%
8	343	$34.28	$1.71	$588	$11,763	11.76%
9	359	$37.02	$1.85	$665	$13,292	13.29%
10	**376**	**$39.98**	**$2.00**	**$751**	**$15,020**	**15.02%**
11	393	$43.18	$2.16	$849	$16,973	16.97%
12	411	$46.63	$2.33	$959	$19,179	19.18%
13	430	$50.36	$2.52	$1,084	$21,673	21.67%
14	450	$54.39	$2.72	$1,225	$24,490	24.49%
15	**471**	**$58.74**	**$2.94**	**$1,384**	**$27,674**	**27.67%**
16	493	$63.44	$3.17	$1,564	$31,271	31.27%
17	516	$68.52	$3.43	$1,767	$35,337	35.34%
18	540	$74.00	$3.70	$1,997	$39,930	39.93%
19	565	$79.92	$4.00	$2,256	$45,121	45.12%
20	**591**	**$86.31**	**$4.32**	**$2,549**	**$50,987**	**50.99%**
21	618	$93.22	$4.66	$2,881	$57,615	57.62%
22	647	$100.68	$5.03	$3,255	$65,105	65.11%
23	677	$108.73	$5.44	$3,678	$73,569	73.57%
24	708	$117.43	$5.87	$4,157	$83,133	83.13%
25	**741**	**$126.82**	**$6.34**	**$4,697**	**$93,940**	**93.94%**
26	775	$136.97	$6.85	$5,308	$106,153	106.15%
27	811	$147.93	$7.40	$5,998	$119,953	119.95%
28	848	$159.76	$7.99	$6,777	$135,546	135.55%
29	888	$172.54	$8.63	$7,658	$153,167	153.17%
30	**929**	**$186.35**	**$9.32**	**$8,654**	**$173,079**	**173.08%**
31	972	$201.25	$10.06	$9,779	$195,579	195.58%
32	1,017	$217.35	$10.87	$11,050	$221,005	221.00%
33	1,064	$234.74	$11.74	$12,487	$249,735	249.74%
34	1,113	$253.52	$12.68	$14,110	$282,201	282.20%
35	**1,165**	**$273.80**	**$13.69**	**$15,944**	**$318,887**	**318.89%**
36	1,219	$295.71	$14.79	$18,017	$360,343	360.34%
37	1,275	$319.36	$15.97	$20,359	$407,187	407.19%
38	1,334	$344.91	$17.25	$23,006	$460,121	460.12%
39	1,396	$372.51	$18.63	$25,997	$519,937	519.94%
40	**1,460**	**$402.31**	**$20.12**	**$29,376**	**$587,529**	**587.53%**

For arguments sake, let's see what happens when we do not reinvest our dividends into more shares of the stock and simply keep the dividends as cash. Referring to table 4.4, we can see that our total value after 40 years (including cash dividends) would be $42,242 after initially investing $2,000. While we still made some decent money, it does not even compare to the $235,012 we would have if we reinvested our dividends.

Table 4.4

Year	Number of Shares	Price	Dividend	Dividend Amount	Total Value	Actual Dividend Yield
1	100	$20.00	$1.00	$100	$2,100	5.00%
2	100	$21.60	$1.08	$108	$2,268	5.40%
3	100	$23.33	$1.17	$117	$2,449	5.83%
4	100	$25.19	$1.26	$126	$2,645	6.30%
5	**100**	**$27.21**	**$1.36**	**$136**	**$2,857**	**6.80%**
6	100	$29.39	$1.47	$147	$3,086	7.35%
7	100	$31.74	$1.59	$159	$3,332	7.93%
8	100	$34.28	$1.71	$171	$3,599	8.57%
9	100	$37.02	$1.85	$185	$3,887	9.25%
10	**100**	**$39.98**	**$2.00**	**$200**	**$4,198**	**10.00%**
11	100	$43.18	$2.16	$216	$4,534	10.79%
12	100	$46.63	$2.33	$233	$4,896	11.66%
13	100	$50.36	$2.52	$252	$5,288	12.59%
14	100	$54.39	$2.72	$272	$5,711	13.60%
15	**100**	**$58.74**	**$2.94**	**$294**	**$6,168**	**14.69%**
16	100	$63.44	$3.17	$317	$6,662	15.86%
17	100	$68.52	$3.43	$343	$7,194	17.13%
18	100	$74.00	$3.70	$370	$7,770	18.50%
19	100	$79.92	$4.00	$400	$8,392	19.98%
20	**100**	**$86.31**	**$4.32**	**$432**	**$9,063**	**21.58%**
21	100	$93.22	$4.66	$466	$9,788	23.30%
22	100	$100.68	$5.03	$503	$10,571	25.17%
23	100	$108.73	$5.44	$544	$11,417	27.18%
24	100	$117.43	$5.87	$587	$12,330	29.36%
25	**100**	**$126.82**	**$6.34**	**$634**	**$13,316**	**31.71%**
26	100	$136.97	$6.85	$685	$14,382	34.24%
27	100	$147.93	$7.40	$740	$15,532	36.98%
28	100	$159.76	$7.99	$799	$16,775	39.94%
29	100	$172.54	$8.63	$863	$18,117	43.14%
30	**100**	**$186.35**	**$9.32**	**$932**	**$19,566**	**46.59%**
31	100	$201.25	$10.06	$1,006	$21,132	50.31%
32	100	$217.35	$10.87	$1,087	$22,822	54.34%
33	100	$234.74	$11.74	$1,174	$24,648	58.69%
34	100	$253.52	$12.68	$1,268	$26,620	63.38%
35	**100**	**$273.80**	**$13.69**	**$1,369**	**$28,749**	**68.45%**
36	100	$295.71	$14.79	$1,479	$31,049	73.93%
37	100	$319.36	$15.97	$1,597	$33,533	79.84%
38	100	$344.91	$17.25	$1,725	$36,216	86.23%
39	100	$372.51	$18.63	$1,863	$39,113	93.13%
40	**100**	**$402.31**	**$20.12**	**$2,012**	**$42,242**	**100.58%**

And looking at the line graphs below, we can see the significant differences in total stock value and the actual dividend yield as time goes on.

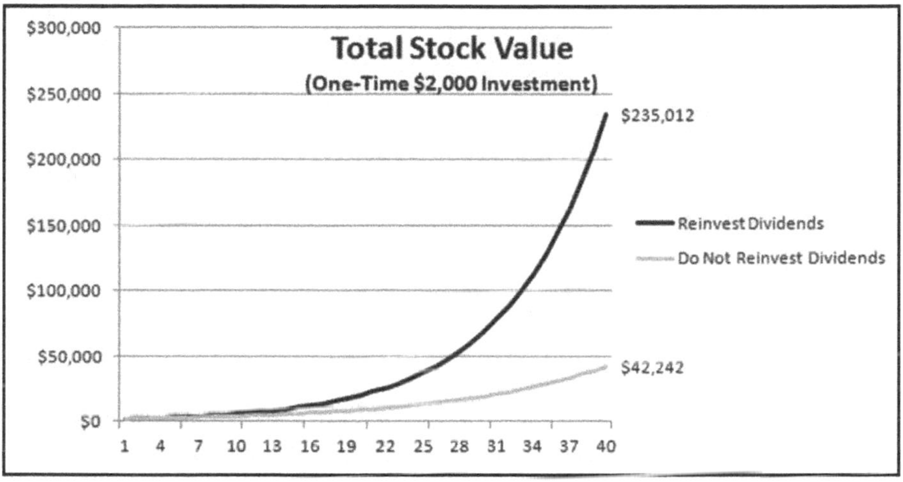

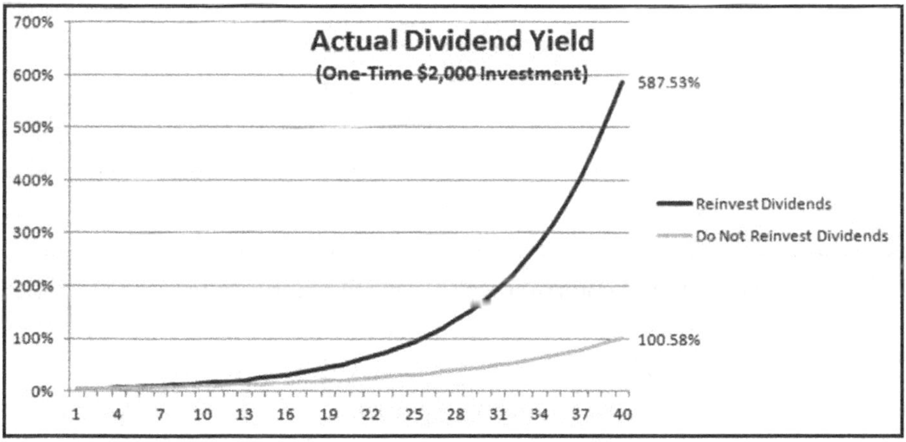

Amazing! After 20 years of investing for myself and managing other people's wealth, I still get excited when talking about dividend reinvesting, compounding, and growing your money. However, it is time to move on.

We have discussed stocks in detail in this chapter, though we have not talked about what causes a stock price to change. Stock prices change due to many variables. Generally speaking, though, there are three major reasons why stock prices go up or down.

- Stock prices change because of supply and demand
- The price movement of the stock indicates what investors feel a company is worth
- Theoretically, a company's earnings are what affects the price of its stock

Reflecting on the third bullet point, the profit a company makes is the main driver of stock prices. There are many times that the price of a stock may go up or down based on other factors. However, stock prices usually will regress at or near its price relevant to its earnings. Many investors have bought stocks based solely on speculation that the company will eventually earn a great deal of profit. Speculation is a very risky investing philosophy. To illustrate this statement, I'd like to discuss a company most of us are familiar with, XM Sirius satellite radio. In case you are unfamiliar with this company, they are the leading producer of the satellite radio business. Satellite radio is a wonderful product that can be found in most new cars, as well as many homes. Satellite radio gives you the ability to tune into specialized radio stations, as well as radio stations all over the country. Not long ago, XM satellite radio and Sirius satellite radio were two different companies. Back in 2005, Sirius satellite radio signed one of the most controversial radio personalities of our time, Howard Stern. At the time the company announced the deal with Howard Stern, Sirius satellite radio's stock price was around $4.00 per share. Almost instantly, the stock doubled in price once the news came out. If you had already owned the stock at the time the announcement was made you would have doubled your money. It never ceases to amaze me how efficient the stock market can be.

Put yourself in this situation. If you owned Sirius satellite radio at the time the stock price doubled, would you have sold it? The easy answer would be "of course I would sell it!" Later on in the book you will see that this is not an easy thing to do. Anyway, I can recall numerous phone calls from friends, family members and clients suggesting that they should buy the stock. What would you have told them? In some ways, it is very easy to tell them they should definitely buy the stock given the fact that the stock price doubled and they signed a high-profile personality. And saying they should buy the stock confirms to them that they were right, which would make them feel very good about themselves. However, ethically speaking, that was not the advice I gave to them. Although I felt I was raining on their parade, I was compelled to explain to them that the stock price doubled mostly due to hype. While the company certainly had an amazing product, and one that was in great demand, they were going to have to pay Howard Stern millions of dollars over the life of his contract. Paying Howard Stern millions of dollars is not of great concern if the company was generating a profit and was sitting on a pile of cash. However, Sirius satellite radio was losing money. And they were losing lots of it. To pay their employees, invest in research and design, and to keep up with demand, they had to borrow millions upon millions of dollars to stay in business. Many small companies find themselves in the same type of situation at some point in their business cycle. This is where a company's earnings come into play relevant to stock prices. Since Sirius satellite radio was not a profitable company, the stock price started trending downward soon after it reached $8.00 per share. Investors began to realize that signing Howard Stern was a huge gamble and might not pay off in the long run. I can remember the price of the stock falling down to less than $1.00 per share. I can tell you that Sirius satellite radio had its first profitable quarter ever a few years ago. That is certainly a positive sign for the company. However, they would have to post positive earnings for many successive quarters thereafter to convey confidence among investors.

The previous story is not uncommon in the investment world. Typically, when a company doubles in price instantly, it will begin a downward trend soon after. This is not to say that every time a stock doubles in price it will definitely trend down soon after, but most times stocks perform this way because of hype and speculation. In the 1990s, many people invested much of their money in dot com companies. This is when the Internet was growing exponentially, but was still in its early stages. Dot com companies were being created by the thousands. The majority of these companies were losing millions of dollars each year. These companies, as well as investors, were speculating that the Internet was the next big thing to drive the economy and they wanted to get in on the ground floor. Investors had total disregard to the financial situation of these companies, especially since almost all of their stocks seemed to be going up in price every day and every year. If we fast forward to March 2001, we will see that the appropriately-named "Dot com Bubble" was short-lived. People started realizing that most of these companies would never be successful and would soon be out of business. Everyone started selling their stocks, which triggered a massive sell-off in the stock market. In just a few weeks' time, most investors lost all of their profits and even most of their money. Some people lost millions of dollars, while other people lost much of their retirement savings. The reason I bring up what happened in March 2001 is not to dissuade you from investing in stocks. The reason I am explaining to you what happened is to prove my point that a company's EARNINGS is what matters most when it comes to stock prices. To be a savvy investor, you need to be disciplined enough to not get caught up in all of the hype and speculation. You need to create an investing plan, implement the plan, revise the plan when necessary, and stick to your guns.

We spent a lot of time discussing exactly what a stock is, how a company becomes public and issues stock, types of stocks, and dividend reinvesting. Since stocks will likely be the majority of your investment portfolio when you are young, you needed to gain a comprehensive understanding of them. In the next chapter, we will make a 180° turn and talk in detail about our next type of investment--bonds.

"Whether you are trying to increase your capital in the short run or the long run, stocks have historically given the greatest return on your investment. Although they tend to be riskier than other investment options, if you do your research on the company, you will find stocks as a successful way of generating more income by taking advantage of compounding and dividend reinvesting."

-Lauren Zawacki, Pennsylvania State University

CHAPTER FIVE

WHY SHOULD I INVEST IN BONDS?

It may appear to you that bonds are extremely boring investments. After all, we know that bonds are generally safe, and therefore less volatile. Though, in all likelihood, we could never become wealthy if we invested all of our money in bonds. However, bonds play an important role in your investment portfolio. In this chapter we will learn how bonds control risk and how they can be a worthwhile investment to buy. We will learn about bond characteristics, types of bonds, interest rates, and bond prices. So let's get started.

A bond is nothing more than a loan of which you are the lender. You receive interest on a loan based on the *coupon* rate of the bond. When the term of the bond ends, the face value of the bond is returned. The face value is the principal or the money you get back when a bond ends, or matures. Bonds are debt and therefore, you are a creditor, where stocks are equity and you are an owner. (This is why stocks are sometimes referred to as equities) The coupon is the amount a bondholder receives as interest payments. The maturity date is the future day in which the investor's principal is repaid. For example, let's assume we invest in a bond that has a face value of $1,000, a coupon rate of 5%, and a maturity date of 10 years. This means we would receive $50 in interest every year for the next 10 years ($1,000 X 5%) for a total of $500. (See Table 5.1) Assuming we invested $1,000 in this bond, we would get our original investment back after the bond matures. It is useful to note that bonds pay interest semi-annually or every six months. So we would actually receive $25 every six months.

Table 5.1

Face Value	Coupon Rate	Years to Maturity	Interest per Year ($1,000 X 5%)	Total Interest Received ($50 x 10 Years)
$1,000	5%	10	$50	$500

Every bond has a credit rating, which helps distinguish a company's or government's credit risk. Let's look into bond credit ratings in more detail before we discuss the types of bonds. Generally speaking, there is less risk in owning bonds than owning stocks. Looking at table 5.2 below, we see that some bonds can be as risky, or even more risky, than some stocks.

Table 5.2

<table>
<tr><th colspan="2">Standard & Poor's Bond Credit Ratings</th></tr>
<tr><td rowspan="5">Investment Grade</td><td>AAA</td></tr>
<tr><td>AA</td></tr>
<tr><td>A</td></tr>
<tr><td>BBB</td></tr>
<tr><td>BBB-</td></tr>
<tr><td rowspan="7">Speculative Grade (Junk Bonds)</td><td>BB+</td></tr>
<tr><td>BB</td></tr>
<tr><td>B</td></tr>
<tr><td>CCC</td></tr>
<tr><td>CC</td></tr>
<tr><td>C</td></tr>
<tr><td>D</td></tr>
</table>

Starting from the top of the chart, the highest quality bond is considered AAA. This means that the company or government is highly unlikely to default on making their interest payments to bondholders. Because high-quality bonds have lower risk, the coupon rates, or the interest that you will receive, will also be lower. Moving down the list, we notice that the further down you go, the riskier the bond will be. You will also notice that BBB- and above would still be considered an *investment grade* bond. Notice that if the company or government falls below BBB-, its grade changes from investment grade quality to speculative or junk bond status. You may have heard the term junk bond before in conversations among adults or investors. When you hear this term, how does it make you feel? Psychologically, most investors would never buy a bond labeled "junk". Most of the time this is justified. However, there is nothing wrong with purchasing junk bonds for your investment portfolio. You will get a much higher coupon rate for taking on the additional risk. Keep in mind that you should keep the amount of junk bonds in your portfolio to a minimum.

A quick side note here. Junk bonds are now called *high-yield* bonds. This is the financial services industry's clever way to disguise some of the risks of junk bonds. Think about it. If your financial advisor came up to you and suggested you put some of your hard-earned money into junk bonds, it would certainly be a hard sell. Conversely, if your financial advisor came up to you and suggested you invest some of your money in high-yield bonds, it would be a much easier sell. High-yield sounds like a wonderful investment where you could make a great amount of money. It is amazing how various marketing strategies also come into play when dealing with various investments.

MAIN TYPES OF BONDS

There are three main types of bonds. The first one we will discuss is a U.S. government bond. US government bonds are extremely safe and, for the most part, AAA rated. The US government has never failed to pay interest on their bonds. US government bonds fall into three categories:

1. **Government Bills** - these bonds mature in less than one year and are considered short-term bonds.
2. **Government Notes** - these bonds mature in one to 10 years and are considered medium-term bonds.
3. **Government Bonds** - these bonds mature in more than 10 years and are considered long-term bonds.

The next type of bond we will discuss is a municipal bond, also known as a muni-bond. Municipal bonds are issued by state and local governments, as well as school districts. These types of bonds help bring in money to pay for anything from roads, parks, infrastructure, and schools. They could also pay for various services such as firefighters, emergency services, and policemen. A huge benefit of investing in municipal bonds is that the earnings you generate from them are free from federal income taxes. This is the first time we have mentioned taxes. While most people do not want to even mention the word 'taxes', they are a necessary evil. Federal income taxes flow to the US government and pays for interstate highways, our armed services, and other benefits we sometimes take for granted. Consequently, federal income taxes are the biggest deduction taken out of your paycheck. You can potentially save money by investing in municipal bonds if you are in a high federal income tax bracket. For example, if your federal income tax bracket is 25%, and you earn $500 in interest from a municipal bond, you will save $125 in taxes ($500 X 25%). Conversely, if you earn $500 in interest from a government bond, you would have to pay $125 in federal income taxes. It's worth noting that when generating earnings from government bonds, you are exempt from state income taxes. Being *exempt* from taxes means that you are not required to pay them. It is also worth noting that state income taxes represent a much lower percentage than federal income taxes. When looking at the state of Pennsylvania, for example, we can see that their state income tax rate is around 3%. This is much lower than the federal income tax rates of most Americans.

The last main type of bond I would like to discuss is the corporate bond. Corporate bonds are issued by companies, not federal, state, or local governments. Corporations issue bonds as a way of borrowing money to pay for various things that will enhance and improve their business. In general, most corporate bonds are riskier than US government bonds and municipal bonds, which results in higher coupon rates. However, the earnings you generate from investing in corporate bonds are fully taxed, both at the federal level and the state level. This brings me to my next question. How do we know whether to buy a corporate bond or a municipal bond? To understand which bond we should invest in at any given point in time, we can look at the following scenario:

Mike is looking at two investment opportunities for bonds. One of the bonds is a corporate bond and has a 7% coupon rate, while the other is a municipal bond that offers a 6% coupon rate. Mike is in the 25% federal income tax bracket. Which bond should Mike purchase?

To make an informed decision on which type of bond Mike should invest in, we can use a calculation called *taxable equivalent yield*, or TEY. Taxable equivalent yield is a simple calculation that will allow us to make a fair comparison between the corporate bond and the municipal bond. Without calculating taxable equivalent yield, we cannot make a fair comparison between these two bonds. The reason is that the corporate bond generates earnings that are taxed, while the earnings from the municipal bond are free from federal income taxes. In the business world this is sometimes called comparing apples to oranges. Since you cannot compare an apple to an orange, we have to convert the orange to an apple! In other words, we are going to use the taxable equivalent yield calculation to convert the municipal bond into a taxable, or corporate bond. The calculation for taxable equivalent yield is as follows:

TEY = Tax Free Rate/(1 – Income Tax rate)

Substituting the numbers in the formula we arrive at the following:

TEY = 6%/(1 – 25%)

TEY = 6%/(75%)

TEY = .06/.75

TEY = .08 or 8%

This means that investing in this municipal bond at 6% is the same as investing in a corporate bond at 8%. In other words, it is not worth paying the taxes on your earnings from the corporate bond. Now we can compare apples to apples because we just converted the tax-free bond into a taxable bond. Previously we were trying to compare a tax-free bond to a taxable bond which is not a fair comparison. Since 8% is higher than 7%, Mike should invest in the municipal bond. This is an important decision to arrive at because it affects how much money you will make on your investment. Remember, knowledge is power.

Fast forward five to ten years when you are likely making significantly more money in your career. Now imagine you have a meeting with your financial advisor. He recommends that you invest some of your money in a new tax-free municipal bond that is paying 4%. He is asking for your permission to put the trade through. What are you going to ask him? Hopefully you are going to ask him what your taxable equivalent yield is at the time and if there is a corporate bond that is worth considering that is paying more than your taxable equivalent yield. If your advisor has no idea what you are talking about, you need to find a new financial advisor! If your advisor does know what you are talking about, he will likely look at you with a surprised stare and realize that he is dealing with a well-informed, knowledgeable client. This is important when working with a financial advisor because he or she will be well aware that you understand a great deal about investing. He or she will know that they will have to be well-prepared when making recommendations to you and that your relationship is more of a partnership rather than a one-sided thought process. Of course the best reason to acquire knowledge about investing is that it can quite possibly save you or make you additional money in your investment portfolio.

YIELD TO MATURITY

The next area of bond investing we need to explore is yield to maturity. As you will see, yield to maturity is really the only thing that matters when investing in a bond in the *secondary market* and holding it until it matures. The secondary market refers to the place where bonds are traded. In fact, it is similar to where we buy and sell (or trade) stocks, except that we are trading bonds. The secondary market, as you may recall from discussing IPOs, is different from the primary market because prices of assets in the secondary market are determined by supply and demand. There is a buyer and seller for every trade that occurs. The primary market is where new issues (whether stocks or bonds) are created and set at a fixed price to be sold to initial investors before hitting the secondary market.

Yield to maturity is an advanced calculation that shows the TOTAL return you will receive if you hold the bond until maturity. Consider these two factors:

1. You can make money from bonds on the interest you receive.
2. You can make or *lose* money from bonds depending on the price of the bond.

Recall that we are referring to the bonds traded in the secondary market when discussing yield to maturity. The yield to maturity of a bond sold in the primary market will always be the same as its coupon rate. Let's take a look at the first factor in the yield to maturity calculation.

The first way to make money from bonds is simply the interest you receive from the company or government every six months. For example, if you invest in one IBM bond that has a 6% coupon rate, a maturity of 7 years, and a total face value of $10,000, you will earn $600 in interest each year for a total of $4,200 in interest over the 7 year period. (See Table 5.3) This is certainly easy to understand and is fairly straightforward. However, when taking into consideration the 2nd factor in the yield to maturity calculation, we realize that it becomes more difficult to understand. Let's move slowly while taking a look at the 2nd factor.

Table 5.3

Total Face Value	Coupon Rate	Years to Maturity	Total Interest Received ($10,000 x 6% x 7 Years)
$10,000	6%	7	$4,200

Bonds are typically priced with a face value of $1,000. There are some exceptions such as United States Savings Bonds that can have various face values. You may very well have received these types of bonds from family members in the past. However, most other bonds you invest in will have a face value of $1,000. Also, recall that bonds trade like stocks in the secondary market. Therefore, the price that you buy or sell a bond at will fluctuate on a daily basis much like stocks. Basically what we are saying is that just because a bond has a face value of $1,000 doesn't mean you are going to pay $1,000 for the bond. In all likelihood, you will be paying more or less for it if you purchase it in the secondary market. This is where it can get a little confusing. So we are going to take a look at a detailed example of how this works.

You are interested in investing in a bond that has a face value of $1,000 and is priced at 105 in the bond market. What this means is that you will have to pay 105% of the face value of the bond. Therefore, this bond would cost you $1,050 ($1,000 x 105%). This is considered buying a bond at a *premium* since you are paying more than its face value. If you keep the bond until it matures, you will receive the face value of the bond, which is $1,000. Most people think that they will receive their $1,050 back, but that is not the case since you paid a premium on the bond. Bond investors will always receive the face value of the bond upon maturity. In this scenario you will **LOSE** $50 on the ***price*** of the bond. Conversely, if this bond had a price of 95, you will only have to pay 95% of the face value of the bond. Therefore, the bond would only cost you $950 ($1,000 x 95%). This is considered buying a bond at a ***discount*** since you are paying less than its face value. If you keep the bond until it matures, you will receive the face value of the bond, which again is $1,000. In this scenario you will **GAIN** $50 on the ***price*** of the bond since you only paid $950 for it.

Okay. Stay with me now as we put it all together regarding yield to maturity. Using the above example, let's assume that the bond has a coupon rate of 4%. That would mean we would receive $40 each year until the bond matures ($1,000 x 4%). However, this does not necessarily mean our investment is giving us a 4% return on our investment. We have to consider the fact that we will either lose money or make money on the price of the bond if held to maturity. Again, this is based on investing in bonds in the secondary market. (I tend to repeat myself at times, but it is an important assumption to remember). Ask yourself this question: Would our percentage return on this investment be higher or lower than 4% if we bought the bond at a premium? Hopefully, you figured out that your return would be lower since you would lose money on the price of the bond. This is why yield to maturity is the only number we look at when investing in bonds in the secondary market and holding them until maturity. It takes into consideration the interest you earn as well as the money you make or lose on the price of the bond. In our example, we lost $50 on the price of the bond so our overall return would certainly be lower even though we are generating 4% interest each year. Another way to look at it is to determine the actual dollar amount we would earn over the life of the bond. If the bond matured in five years, we would generate $200 in total interest over the five years. That is certainly a decent amount of interest earned. Now take into consideration the fact that we lost $50 on the price of the bond and we can see that we really only made $150 in total. (See Table 5.4) Therefore, aside from yield to maturity, nothing else matters regarding the amount of return you will receive at maturity. Of course you will still have to consider the bond rating, taxable equivalent yield, and other factors in the decision-making process. With regard to your percentage return, however, yield to maturity tells the entire story with just one number to consider.

Table 5.4

Face Value of Bond	Coupon Rate	Years to Maturity	Total Interest Received	Cash Paid for Bond	Loss on Price of Bond ($1,050 - $1,000)	Total Gain ($200 - $50)
$1,000	4%	5	$200	$1,050	$50	$150

Here is one more example of yield to maturity: A corporate bond is paying an 8.5% coupon rate, is currently priced at around 150, and has a maturity of about ten years. (At the time of this writing, this was an actual corporate bond that was available in the bond market) Many people will become excited over this bond because it is paying 8.5%, which is quite good. Savvy investors, however, will realize that they would be paying a large premium for this bond. Consequently, the yield to maturity for this bond was just 2.73%! That means that if you invested in this bond and held it until maturity you would earn a 2.73% total return on your investment per year, not 8.5%. That is certainly a significant difference.

BOND PRICES AND INTEREST RATE MOVEMENTS

What makes a bond price go up or down? Bond prices and interest rates move in opposite directions. This is a fundamental concept that helps us understand price trends in bonds.

- When bond prices rates go down, interest rates go up.
- When bond prices go up, interest rates go down.

To help us grasp this concept, let's discuss the state of interest rates as of this writing (March 2014). Interest rates in March 2014 were at historical lows, but were beginning to creep up. There are many reasons why they were ridiculously low, but that discussion is out of the realm of the concepts in this book. However, we can take a look at an example of how and why bond prices move in opposite directions when compared to interest rate movements.

Imagine yourself in the not so far future. You are interested in diversifying your portfolio by adding bonds to it. One corporate bond, in particular, is paying a 3% interest rate and has a maturity of 10 years. The bond is a new issue, and therefore, you are purchasing it at par value (100) in the primary market. You decide to invest $10,000 in this bond. Now you have 10 bonds in your investment portfolio valued at $1,000 each, and paying you 3% in interest each year. Three years later, interest rates have trended upward. At this time, the corporation that issued your bonds decides to issue additional bonds. The new bonds that the corporation decides to issue also have a maturity date of 10 years. However, since interest rates have gone up, the coupon rate for the new bonds is 5%. At the same time, you strongly consider selling your bonds in the secondary market because you are rebalancing your portfolio to bring you back to your proper asset allocation. This means that you have to go out into the bond market to try and sell your bonds. Remember, your bonds have a 3% coupon rate and the new bonds are paying 5%. Therefore, assuming the price of the bonds were the same, would a buyer of bonds buy a bond that pays 5% or 3%? Obviously, bond investors would buy the bonds that are paying 5%. For arguments sake, we were assuming the price of the bonds were identical in order to understand the concept. In reality, the prices of these bonds would never be the same given their different coupon rates. What do you think would happen to the price of the bond that is only paying 3%? The correct answer is that the price of this bond would certainly go down to a level that would entice bond investors to buy. This is why bond prices will go down when interest rates go up. Conversely, this is why bond prices will go up when interest rates go down. Additionally, the above scenario helps us further understand the concept of yield to maturity. Since the price of the 3% of bond would go down, investors who bought this bond would be paying a discount to purchase it. Consequently, they would make money on the price of the bond. Therefore, the yield to maturity would be higher than 3%.

Now that we have a good understanding of how bond prices fluctuate, we can discuss ideal times to invest in bonds. Since interest rates were at historic lows in March 2014, would it have been an ideal time to invest in bonds? Generally speaking, certainly not! However, this does not mean I would not have recommended bonds for certain clients. If a particular bond was appropriate at the time for their portfolio and helped them achieve their goals it would be a good investment.

Why was March 2014 not a good time to buy bonds? Recall that when interest rates are low bond prices are high. Therefore, if you bought a bond in March 2014 you would have paid a high price for the bond and received a low interest rate. Assuming you bought a bond that matured in ten years, you would have been stuck with receiving low interest payments for that period of time. Furthermore, when interest rates finally rise (and they always will eventually), you will be locked in to your high-priced, low interest rate bond. If you decide to sell the bond you will soon realize that you will likely have to sell it at a steep discount. This unfortunate situation is often called ***interest rate risk***. There are various ways to reduce interest rate risk, but a simple solution would be to buy shorter-term bonds. Buying shorter-term bonds would alleviate the risk because your bonds would soon mature, which would allow you to receive your principal back and invest your money in newer bonds with a higher interest rate. In March 2014 I would have recommended bonds that had a maturity date of no more than five years, and in most cases no more than three years.

Another way to alleviate interest rate risk is to construct a *laddered* bond portfolio. An example of a laddered bond portfolio would be to invest in various bonds that mature in one, two, three, four, and five years. Every year you would have some of your bonds mature which would allow you to take the principal and invest in five year bonds. If interest rates **rise** to historic levels, you could always take your principal and shift it into longer-term bonds. There are many ways to construct bond portfolios that would help reduce interest-rate risk, but the two suggestions above are easy to implement and usually provide good results.

It is important to understand the implications interest rates have on your investment decisions. Being an informed investor will help you make appropriate choices for bonds in your portfolio and will help maximize your returns. There are many sources of information on the Internet that can provide current interest rate data, such as Bankrate.com and Marketwatch.com, which contain updated information about key interest rates. Another useful website is www.federalreserve.gov/monetarypolicy, which provides detailed statements about where interest rates may be heading and if/when the Federal Reserve will raise or lower rates.

To many young investors bonds are considered a "boring" investment. As discussed in this chapter, however, bonds are necessary for our portfolios because it manages risk and helps us maintain a proper asset allocation. When stocks fall, bonds *usually* rise, which stresses the importance of having a well-allocated portfolio. Bonds also provide much needed income in our retirement years by replacing our income we were making throughout our careers. While we spent much time discussing bonds, you now have a greater understanding of how and when to buy them, their role in your investment plan, and why they are necessary in building and maintaining wealth. In the next chapter we will learn about mutual funds and what role they will have in your portfolio.

"While stocks may be a more exciting and lucrative means of saving money and increasing capital, it is important to decrease your risk while investing. Bonds are a great source of low-risk, steady income that are vital to a balanced portfolio."

-Bryan Welch, UCLA

CHAPTER SIX

MUTUAL FUNDS & ETFs

Imagine yourself at your first significant job out of college. You were hired by an accounting firm as a junior analyst and you are excited about beginning your career. Six months into your job you receive a thick packet in your mailbox at work that is titled '401k Retirement Plan Information'. You curiously open the packet and find many documents that contain large and small print that you are dreading reading. After reluctantly turning each page you realize that it is probably a good idea to begin investing some of your hard-earned money into the plan for various reasons that we will discuss in a later chapter. Suddenly you discover a list of investments called 'mutual funds' and learn that you can only purchase these types of investments within your 401k plan. Never having learned anything about mutual funds, you proceed to ask some of your colleagues which mutual funds would be good choices. Your colleagues basically instruct you to simply choose any of them and that it doesn't really matter. Walking back to your desk, confused and disappointed, you magically recall that you discovered a book a while ago on how to become wealthy. With a renewed sense of enthusiasm, you eagerly sift through all of your books collecting dust on your bookshelf and find 'The Early Investor' begging to be read. You turn off all of your electronic devices so no one can interrupt you from your personal reading time. You are well on your way to learning this vital information you can use to help learn about mutual funds and to make informed decisions in your retirement plan. The following information details the interesting and helpful information that you found.

A mutual fund is an investment that contains a pool of money from numerous investors for the purpose of investing in assets such as stocks, bonds, and cash investments. For example, some mutual funds can have hundreds of different stocks or bonds within the fund. When you invest in a mutual fund, you are investing in a piece of all the stocks, bonds, and other investments within the fund. There are obvious advantages and some not so obvious advantages of mutual funds.

Advantages:

- Gives accessibility to various investments to small investors
- In theory, professional management
- Diversification
- Liquidity
- Simplicity

Mutual funds have the unique ability to allow investors who do not have a large amount of money to participate in the stock and bond markets. There are many mutual fund companies such as Vanguard, Fidelity, Oppenheimer, and T. Rowe Price that will allow you to invest in their mutual funds for as little as $50 per month or in some cases less. These companies make it easy to open an account and choose which funds you want to purchase. You will likely be required to set up an automatic investment plan where your monthly payment into your account is taken out of your savings or checking account. The automatic monthly payment into your plan will be taken out at the same time each month and invested according to the mutual fund or funds you choose. This is also a form of dollar-cost averaging!

Another advantage of mutual funds is that many of them are managed professionally. These professional managers invest your money in various investments that they feel will perform well. For example, the manager may decide that he is going to purchase Apple stock within the fund. He may also decide to sell certain investments that he feels may not rise any further or even ones that are trending downward. Professional managers are well-educated and have experience in analyzing specific investments that they feel will do well in their mutual fund portfolio. They also have a team of analysts that work under them who can search and discover opportunities in financial markets. Most investors, small and large, young and old, do not have the education, experience or tools to analyze and choose investments that are appropriate for their investment portfolios.

Diversification is one of the greatest advantages of mutual funds. Imagine you have $10,000 to invest. You are considering investing the money in one stock or investing the money in a mutual fund. It is interesting to see what might happen in each of these investments. Let's start with our first choice--investing the money in one stock. After purchasing the stock with your $10,000 you cannot help feeling excited. After all, your Investment Management teacher, Mr. Zisa, would constantly preach to you about starting to invest, and now that day has finally come! A few months later, the company you invested in comes out with some really bad news. Consequently, the stock price goes down an unimaginable 80%, which means you only have $2,000 left from your investment! (See Table 6.1) Hopefully after reading this book you will not invest in a company that carries a great deal of risk like the fictitious one above. However, in theory, any stock can go down a great deal in a short amount of time.

Table 6.1

Money Invested in One Stock	% Decline in Stock Price	Current Value of Stock	Current Investment Loss
$10,000	80%	$2,000	$8,000

Now let's see what might happen when investing the $10,000 in a mutual fund. For simplicity's sake, assume that the mutual fund you purchase is invested equally in 100 stocks. If one of those stocks falls 80% in value and the remaining 99 stocks are relatively stable, it will not significantly affect you. As a matter of fact, you probably will not see a huge difference in the value of your mutual fund. (See Table 6.2) This is because the mutual fund contains 99 other stocks that provide diversity and help reduce risk within the portfolio. As a young investor it may be a good idea to start investing in mutual funds so that you do not risk losing most or all of your money in one stock. Psychologically, losing most of your money after investing for the first time will cause you to have negative feelings regarding the stock market and may prevent you from becoming wealthy in the long run. If we turn the situation around, we can see that if you invest in one company whose stock price rises dramatically in a short period of time, we could also make a ton of money! If one stock rises dramatically within a mutual fund we will likely not see big difference once again for the same reasons as above. Diversification reduces risk and therefore can also reduce the amount of your return.

Table 6.2

Money Invested in Mutual Fund	% Decline in One Stock	Current Value of Mutual Fund	Current Investment Loss
$10,000	80%	$9,920	$80

The next advantage of a mutual fund is that it is a very liquid investment. If you need to access the money in your mutual fund investment, it is very easy to sell. Not quite as easy as selling a stock, but the results are very similar. When selling a stock, you simply put a sell order in through your financial advisor or through an online trading account. We will discuss brokers and online trading in Chapter 10. In most cases, once you submit your sell order, the trade will execute immediately and the cash proceeds will be readily available. When selling a mutual fund, you also put a sell order in through your financial advisor or through your online trading account. However, the mutual fund will not be sold until the end of the trading day, 4:00 P.M. EST. Upon the sale of your mutual fund the cash proceeds will again be readily available. Now you can see why mutual funds are highly liquid. It is rather easy to convert mutual fund investments into cash.

The last advantage of a mutual fund is its simplicity. Due to its characteristics, you do not need a lot of time and experience to invest in them. That is one of the major reasons why most investors will only invest in mutual funds. Many people do not have the time or are simply not interested in analyzing, choosing, and managing their investment portfolio. It is for these reasons that most investors will never purchase individual stocks, individual bonds, or other types of investments. However, investing in mutual funds alone does not necessarily translate into great wealth, as you will see in the next few paragraphs.

Although there are many advantages of mutual funds we cannot overlook some of the disadvantages.

Disadvantages:

- Professional management!!
- Costs
- Diversification!!
- Taxes

How can professional management be a disadvantage to investing in mutual funds? Didn't we just learn that professional management is one of the main advantages of mutual funds? Well, I did not list professional management as a disadvantage to confuse you. I simply want to make you aware that not all professional managers will have good performance numbers in their mutual fund. In fact, many mutual funds that are run by professional money managers do not beat the returns of the S&P 500 over a long period of time. There are many reasons for this that we will begin discussing in the next paragraph. There *are* some mutual funds that perform better than the S&P 500 over a long period of time. However, it does suggest that some professional money managers are not as good as they claim.

One of the reasons many mutual funds have lower returns than the general stock market is that they can cost you a large amount of money to own. Many professional money managers earn a lucrative salary and generate huge bonuses on a yearly basis. What is interesting, or for lack of a better word, discouraging, is that if the mutual fund performs poorly in a given year, professional money managers and their team of analysts still get paid very well. I do not want to seem like I am picking on money managers because there are many who manage mutual funds that consistently perform better than the overall market. I do, however, want to make you aware of the costs involved in owning a mutual fund and how they could erode some of your gains. The cost of a mutual fund is expressed in what we call the *expense ratio*. To put it simply the expense ratio is the ongoing annual expenses of a mutual fund which include:

- The cost of the fund manager
- Administrative costs
- 12 B-1 fees

The ongoing expenses listed above may or may not include other items such as commissions, operating expenses, marketing fees, and trading fees. It is also useful to know that the average expense ratio is somewhere around 1.5%. Why is this important to us? Well, imagine that our mutual fund has a return of 8% in a given year without taking into consideration any of the expenses that we as shareholders have to pay. Now imagine that the expense ratio of this fund is 1.5%. In reality, we have not made 8% that year. We have only made 6.5% due to the expense ratio. For many people 1.5%

might not sound like a large expense to pay when taking into consideration all the advantages we get from a mutual fund. However, over a long period of time, the ongoing expenses of a mutual fund will eat into our gains and force us to invest for a longer period of time to achieve our goals. There are some mutual funds that charge as much as 3% for their expense ratio! Still, other types of investments can charge much more than 3%, such as hedge funds. I certainly would not mind paying a high expense ratio if I was confident I would achieve a consistently good return over a long period of time. In my experience, however, it is difficult to find mutual funds or other types of investments that outperform the general stock market when charging high fees.

The next disadvantage we need to discuss is diversification. Wait a minute! Again, I thought we said this was an advantage of a mutual fund? Diversification certainly can be a huge advantage when investing in mutual funds, but how can it be a disadvantage? To illustrate how diversification can be a disadvantage, I will explain to you what typically happens at initial meetings I conduct with prospective clients.

When I meet with potential clients for the first time, I usually ask them to show me their latest investment statements. That way I can better assess their financial situation and come up with an appropriate plan and recommendations that will help them achieve their financial goals. Upon looking at their statements, many of them own numerous mutual funds. Usually they own between eight and ten mutual funds, and sometimes more! Since there are many types of mutual funds, some which we will discuss later, there is nothing wrong with owning a wide variety of them. However, eight or more can be excessive. Consider the fact that many mutual funds have over 100 stocks and/or bonds in them. Some mutual funds can contain over 1,000 stocks and/or bonds! If you own eight or more mutual funds, you could own upwards of 5,000 stocks and/or bonds! That is why diversification can be a disadvantage when investing in mutual funds. In other words, you could easily be *over-diversified*, meaning you will never lose a significant amount of your investment, but you will likely generate extremely low returns. It is also highly likely that there is much overlap between some of the stocks and bonds found in a mutual fund portfolio that consists of eight or more mutual funds. For example, one or more of the funds could have Microsoft stock in it. Still other funds could contain identical bonds among them.

The last major disadvantage with mutual funds is related to taxes. Most teenagers will not be overly concerned with taxes until they begin making a significant amount of money. At that point in time, taxes could take a big chunk of money out of your net pay (also known as take-home pay). When making money from investments, we usually have to pay taxes on what we earn, unless the earnings were generated within a tax-advantaged account (We will learn about tax-advantaged accounts later). This applies to mutual funds because as the fund managers buy and sell stock they can produce capital gains. For example, if they bought a stock for $50 per share and the stock price went up to $70 per share, they could decide to sell it and take the profit. That would generate a capital gain of $20 per share. If they bought and sold 100,000 shares, the capital gain generated would be $2,000,000 (100,000 shares multiplied by $20 per share). At the end of the year mutual funds are required to distribute any capital gains they may have to all shareholders. Shareholders of the fund will then be required to pay taxes based on how much they received in capital gains distributions. While having capital gains within a mutual fund is certainly a positive, it does mean that shareholders will have to pay taxes based on how much in capital gains they have received. The main point we need to understand is that mutual fund money managers have no idea what your personal tax situation may be. Again, I realize that most teenagers do not have any tax concerns right now, but that will change sooner than you think. Taxes become a necessary evil when producing wealth. It is beneficial to grow your money through investing, but you should learn how to manage your tax situation. Mutual fund managers cannot manage their portfolio of investments according to your personal tax situation, and, therefore, could cause you to owe a large amount of money to the Internal Revenue Service (IRS). For your information, the IRS is responsible for the collection of tax payments and to make sure individuals and businesses pay their fair share.

HOW CAN WE EARN MONEY FROM MUTUAL FUNDS?

We can earn money by investing in mutual funds in three ways:

1. By earning dividends
2. By receiving capital gains distributions
3. By selling your mutual funds for a profit

There are many mutual funds that pay what is called a *yield*. For example, if a mutual fund pays a yield of 3% and you invest $5,000 in the fund, you will receive $150 ($5,000 x 3%) in dividends. These dividends are distributed from the income generated through dividends on stocks and interest on bonds and cash. This differs from receiving dividends from individual stocks. If you own an individual stock that pays a 4% dividend, you will receive 4%. You can be certain it will be 4% unless the company decides to lower, raise, or get rid of its dividend. However, that is not the case with mutual funds. Since there can be numerous stocks, bonds, and other types of investments within the fund, you receive a specific percentage based on the total income generated from the fund.

Recall that mutual funds pay capital gains distributions. While you will have to pay taxes on the distributions (unless they are generated within a tax-advantaged account), it is still a good way to earn money investing in mutual funds. Occasionally, there will be years where you will receive little or no capital gains due to significant drops in the overall stock and/or bond markets. In 2001 and in 2008, many mutual funds did not have any capital gains. Instead, they generated capital losses due to the terrible economy during those years.

The last way to earn money when investing in mutual funds is to simply sell it for a profit if the fund has gone up in value. If you buy a mutual fund for $30 per share and you sell it for $40 per share, you made a profit of $10 per share. This is similar to buying a stock and selling it for a profit. The only difference is that you buy and sell a mutual fund at its *Net Asset Value* or NAV. NAV is the total assets of the fund minus its total liabilities. Essentially we can think of NAV as the price per share of the mutual fund. When you buy a mutual fund you pay the NAV plus any sales fees. When you sell a mutual fund you receive the current NAV less any sales fees.

TYPES OF MUTUAL FUNDS

There are many types of mutual funds, but there are three main categories:

1. Equity Funds
2. Fixed-Income Funds
3. Money-Market Funds

Equity funds are just stock funds and only contain a variety of stocks within them. Most equity funds will keep a very small percentage in cash as well. Fixed-income funds are bond funds and only contain a variety of bonds within them. Fixed-income funds also may keep some of the fund's assets in cash. Money-market funds consist of short-term investments such as United States Treasury Bonds which translates into a safe place to hold the cash portion of your portfolio. You will not have to worry as much about losing your principal and you will receive a rate of return higher than that of a savings account and similar to rates on certificate of deposits.

While the above types of mutual funds fulfill the major investment categories (stocks, bonds, and cash), there is quite a large selection of other types of funds such as:

- Balanced Funds
- Global/International Funds
- Specialty Funds
- Index Funds

A balanced mutual fund is almost like a one-stop shop. It invests in stocks, bonds, and cash instruments to achieve its objective of providing a mixture of growth, income, and safety. Sometimes balanced funds are referred to as *asset allocation funds*. Asset allocation funds are basically structured in the same way when compared to balanced funds except that asset allocation funds can change the percentage of stocks, bonds, and other investments that they own as the managers see fit.

Although subtle, there is a difference between global and international mutual funds. Global funds invest in companies all over the world, including the United States. International funds invest in companies all over the world, except the United States.

Specialty mutual funds invest in specific segments of the economy, or sector. For example, you can invest in mutual funds that consist of all technology companies. You can invest in mutual funds that consist of all financial companies, pharmaceutical companies, or telecommunication companies. The advantage of a specialty fund is that you can achieve higher gains when compared to other mutual funds because if that sector significantly rises, most or all of the stocks within the fund will rise as well. This will obviously result in more dramatic gains. The downside to investing in specialty funds is that you are less diversified than other mutual funds, which increases your risk and causes you to be susceptible to a specific industry. Another example of a specialty fund is a socially-responsible fund. A unique feature of socially-responsible funds is that they only invest in companies that are good for society and the environment and adhere to certain beliefs of the investor. Socially-responsible funds will not invest in certain industries such as tobacco, alcoholic beverages, weapons, nuclear power, and even some chemical companies.

Index funds are another type of mutual fund that we need to spend some time discussing in greater detail. First, let's define the term *index*. An index is a statistical measure of the changes in a portfolio of stocks, or other investments, representing a segment of the overall market. Essentially an index is just a list of investments. Some of the major stock indexes include:

- DJIA (Dow Jones Industrial Average)
- S&P 500 (Standard & Poor's 500 Index)
- Nasdaq Composite Index
- Wilshire 5000 Total Market Index
- Russell 2000 Index

The Dow Jones Industrial Average is the oldest index which consists of 30 companies known as "blue chips" that have a long history of consistent earnings and have an excellent reputation for delivering profit in both good and bad economic times. Furthermore, the 30 companies in the DJIA are considered leaders in their respective industries. For these reasons, the DJIA is perceived as an index that appeals to investors with a low tolerance for risk. Sometimes a company in the DJIA can be replaced, but this does not happen often. As of September 2015, the DJIA was comprised of the following companies:

3M	General Electric	Nike
American Express	Goldman Sachs Group	Pfizer
Apple	Home Depot	Procter & Gamble
Boeing	IBM	Traveler's
Caterpillar	Intel	UnitedHealth Group
Chevron Corporation	Johnson & Johnson	United Technologies
Cisco Systems	JPMorgan Chase	Verizon Communications
Coca-Cola	McDonald's	Visa
DuPont	Merck	Wal-Mart
ExxonMobil	Microsoft	Walt Disney

One of the observations when looking at the companies listed in the DJIA is the diverse representation of industries, which is another reason that it is considered a lower-risk index. Furthermore, since these companies generate consistent earnings, they generally pay solid dividends.

The S&P 500 is a broader index that lists the 500 most widely held companies in the United States and therefore is considered to be one of the better measurements on how the overall market is doing on a daily, monthly, and annual basis. Because it contains 500 companies, it is well-diversified and accounts for a large percentage of the U.S. stock market. It is also the index that many investors use to compare their investment portfolio performance against and provides a benchmark for mutual fund managers. All of the stocks listed in the Dow Jones Industrial Average can be found in the S&P 500 as well.

The Nasdaq Composite Index contains over 3,000 companies, but many are technology, Internet, and smaller companies. Technology and Internet companies tend to be more volatile given the nature of their businesses. Consequently, the Nasdaq is considered to be an index that is riskier and is watched by investors that have a higher risk tolerance. Conversely, the Nasdaq lists companies that have the potential to grow at a much faster pace when compared to the Dow Jones Industrial Average.

The Wilshire 5000 Total Market Index is a list of almost every public company in the United States and is thus the most diversified index around. However, because it only lists stocks from the United States, there are many foreign companies that are left out, not unlike the other indexes we have discussed so far. It is interesting to note that the Wilshire 5000 actually lists over 6,000 companies, unlike its name would suggest.

The Russell 2000 Index consists of 2,000 of the smaller companies in the United States that have high growth potential. In periods of good economic times, companies within the Russell 2000 will experience above-average gains in the stock market. Conversely, when economic times are tough, many of these smaller stocks fall dramatically and may even go out of business. The main reason that smaller companies have significant issues in a bad economy is because it is much more difficult to have enough available cash to make it through a rough period. Larger companies can withstand tougher economic times because they usually have a broader range of goods and services to fall back on, and certainly have more cash in reserves for emergency purposes.

Other indexes include non-U.S. indexes and industry or sector indexes. Non-U.S. indexes are available in all of the major countries in the world. For example, the Nikkei is Japan's main index, the FTSE is London's main index, and the DAX is Germany's main index. Sector indexes are simply indexes that list companies from a specific industry. There are sector indexes for almost all industries including, but not limited to, healthcare, retail, utilities, education, financial services, transportation, and even mining.

Index funds are just mutual funds! There are hundreds of indexes and hundreds of index funds. However, there are a few important facts about investing in index funds:

- They are *passively* managed, not *actively* managed
- They have lower fees/expenses than actively managed mutual funds
- Most actively managed mutual funds do NOT perform better than passively managed mutual funds

Think of what passively managed versus actively managed could mean relevant to mutual funds. Remember that most mutual funds have managers that buy and sell investments within their fund for the benefit of the shareholder. Also, recall that these managers and their team get paid quite a bit of money to manage their fund. This is why mutual funds that are managed on a day to day basis are considered *actively* managed. Now think about an index fund and how it operates. We have learned that index funds simply represent and track a particular index. Would an index fund require day to day management like an actively managed fund? Of course not! There is no need for a management team because the purpose of an index fund is to simply perform exactly like its index that it tracks. Therefore, index funds are considered to be passively managed. We know that ALL mutual funds have an expense ratio which includes costs for the fund managers, advertising and other expenses. Since index funds are passively managed, their expense ratios are much lower than actively managed funds. Lower expense ratios can translate into higher returns for us because the fund expenses do not eat into our gains. It is astonishing to realize that many actively managed funds do not beat the overall returns of the stock market over a long period of time! One of the main reasons is because of their high expense ratios, although certainly not the only reason. Many actively managed funds might perform better in some years, but be careful you do not chase the latest and so-called greatest investment because it had one or two stellar years. I would choose a mutual fund which consistently returned decent numbers over a ten-year period or longer rather than one which had 1-2 years of huge gains.

After touting index mutual funds in the previous section, I do need to mention that there are some actively managed funds that have beaten the market over a long period of time. Reputable actively managed mutual fund companies include Oppenheimer, American, Pimco, and Franklin Templeton among others. Furthermore, it is important to note that all mutual fund companies have their share of quality funds as well as funds that do not perform well over the long run. The challenge is that it is very difficult for the average investor to discover them since most people do not understand what to look for when doing their analysis. That is why most investors should only invest in index funds unless they have a broad understanding of how to select other types of mutual funds that have outperformed them over a ten year or more period of time. The process of finding these funds is beyond the scope of this book, but nonetheless, the most important criteria to remember is to find steady performing mutual funds that do not have a significantly high expense ratio that would eat into your gains. Keep in mind that this is just the start to finding good actively managed mutual funds.

MUTUAL FUND SHARE CLASSES

When you invest in a mutual fund, you have a choice of which share class you would like to purchase. Although there are many types of mutual fund share classes, the main ones are listed below:

- A shares
- B shares
- C shares

Highlights of an 'A' share:

- ✓ Front-load sales charge
- ✓ Lowest expense ratio of all the main share classes
- ✓ Commission to broker paid up front with small trail (usually .25%)

To help explain a *front-load sales charge*, it is useful to look at a real-life example:

Mike wants to invest $15,000 into ABCD mutual fund. He decides he wants purchase the 'A' share class of the fund. The front-load sales charge on the mutual fund is 4%. How much are his shares worth the instant he buys them?

This is an interesting question because it is not asking us "how much will we be paying in sales charges", but rather "because we are purchasing 'A' shares, what will happen to our $15,000 the moment we purchase this mutual fund". The solution is rather simple and can be seen in Table 6.3 below. It is also important to note that some 'A' share mutual funds can potentially charge a sales load of up to 6% or, in some instances, even more.

Table 6.3

Investment in 'A' Share Mutual Fund	Front-Load Sales Charge %	Sales Charge (in Dollars)	Beginning Value of Mutual Fund
$15,000	4%	$600	$14,400

There is an even easier way to find out that the answer is $14,400. Simply multiply $15,000 by 96%, or .96, to get the answer in one step. The 96% comes from taking 100% of the initial investment and subtracting out 4% in sales charges. While certainly not rocket science, it is useful to start thinking in this way when it pertains to investing and other financial topics. Calculators are obviously good to use in certain situations, but actually using your brain once in a while can be quite stimulating!

'A' share mutual funds carry the distinction of having the lowest expenses of all the main share classes. As we learned when discussing expense ratios, lower cost mutual funds can have a great advantage over ones with higher expenses, especially if you are a long-term investor. Aside from paying a front-load sales charge, there is a small *commission* trail of .25% that you must pay each year following the first year you own the 'A' share mutual fund. A *commission* is the money the investment broker or salesperson receives in earnings when selling you an investment. A front-load sales charge is considered a commission. In the example above, Mike paid $600 in front-load sales charges so his mutual fund shares were worth $14,400 right from the start. Every year thereafter he owns this mutual fund he will be charged a .25% commission based on the value of the fund. For example, if the value of his mutual fund rises to $17,000 in year 3, he will have to pay approximately $42.50 ($17,000 x .25%) in commission that year. The actual number may fluctuate depending on when the .25% is charged and other timing issues, but you should understand the concept now.

Highlights of a 'B' share:

- ✓ Back-load deferred sales charge
- ✓ Highest expense ratio of all the main share classes
- ✓ Highest commission to broker paid up front with small trail (usually .25%)

A back-load sales charge is a harder concept to grasp so we should consider it a small challenge. When investing in 'B' share mutual funds, your initial investment will have the same value even after the moment you place the trade, unlike 'A' shares where the front-load sales charge is taken from the value right away. Therefore, in our previous example, Mike's $15,000 would still be worth $15,000 right from the start. This is definitely a positive when owning 'B' share mutual funds. Unfortunately, there are no more positives to talk about when discussing 'B' shares. When owning 'B' shares, the mutual fund company 'forces' you to own your mutual fund for a specific period of time. They could expect you to own your fund anywhere from three to 8 years and sometimes longer. If you sell your mutual fund before the required time elapses, you will be charged an enormous *back-end sales charge.* These back-end sales charges vary among mutual fund companies, but one thing you can be sure of is that it will be a significant amount. This is why I used the term 'forces' a few sentences ago. You can certainly sell your 'B' share mutual fund anytime, but you will be penalized. There is, however, one exception to the evil rules of the 'B' share mutual fund. You may switch your 'B' share mutual fund to a different 'B' share mutual fund within the same fund family. For example, if you buy a 'B' share mutual fund in the American Funds family you can switch it to another 'B' mutual fund within American Funds at any time without being charged a back-end sales charge. Finally, if you own a 'B' share fund long enough to not be assessed the back-end sales charge your shares will automatically convert to 'A' shares.

Highlights of a 'C' share:

- ✓ Minimum back-load deferred sales charge
- ✓ Highest expense ratio than 'A' share mutual funds
- ✓ Commission to broker level at 1% of the value of the fund each year

'C' share mutual funds are somewhat of a combination between 'A' and 'B' shares. Similar to 'B' shares, 'C' share mutual funds do not charge a front-end sales charge, so your $15,000 is still worth $15,000 the moment you make the purchase. Unlike 'B' shares, you only have to own 'C' share mutual funds for one year for the company to waive the back-load deferred sales charge.

This is not a major concern since most investors are going to own a mutual fund for at least one year. Expense ratios for 'C' share funds can be very high just like 'B' shares so that is something to take into consideration. The investment broker or salesperson earns a flat 1% each year on the value of the mutual fund.

Having learned the differences between the three main share classes, which one would you prefer when investing in mutual funds? Certainly not an easy answer for most of us, but we *can* shed some light on this intriguing question. In general, if you own an 'A' share mutual fund for longer than eight or nine years you will end up paying less in expenses and will generate higher returns than 'B' or 'C' shares. While you may own some funds for a long period of time, there may be instances where you deem it necessary to sell some of your mutual funds for various reasons. One reason might be to rebalance your portfolio. We will discuss rebalancing in detail later on in the book, but it generally means to shift some of your investments into other investments for the purpose of maximizing your returns while minimizing your risk. Therefore, 'A' shares may not be the best choice when planning to rebalance periodically. Imagine if every time you had to sell some of your 'A' share funds to buy new 'A' share funds you had to pay another front-load sales charge. This is definitely a losing methodology to use when investing. Investing in 'C' shares, however, would allow you to begin rebalancing after one year without incurring the front-end sales charges. Yes, your expense ratio will be higher, but that will be more than offset by not having to pay the front-end sales charges each time you rebalance.

It is difficult to find an ideal situation where 'B' share mutual funds would be appropriate for an investment portfolio. I have a hard time justifying the fact that any stockbroker or financial advisor would recommend 'B' shares. I am sure there are investment professionals out there that would argue this point. In fact, I have heard some of their arguments and still cannot ethically state that they would be appropriate in any way, shape, or form. Having said this, I would like to share a story with you related to 'B' share mutual funds.

In the early 2000s while working as a financial advisor for Merrill Lynch, a retired elderly couple came to see me at my office. The husband and wife were retired librarians from a prestigious Ivy League school. Do you think they had much money to invest? Absolutely they did! In fact, they showed me one of their investment account statements which consisted of $500,000 in investments. On the other hand, the $500,000 was invested in four 'B' share mutual funds which the retired couple knew nothing about. They proceeded to tell me that a financial specialist from a local bank recommended the funds about six months prior to our meeting. It seems that the financial specialist wasn't so special after all because he failed to disclose any information regarding the share class he was throwing their money into. After politely listening to their story, I cautiously explained to them the highlights of 'B' share mutual funds. They were literally in tears, especially since the actual funds they were told to invest in were not investments that I would have recommended by any means. By the way, the commission of the wonderful *financial specialist* (the inappropriate title of that person) the day he invested their money was likely in the neighborhood of $25,000! In the financial services world today he would most likely lose his licenses to sell investments, pay huge fines, and possibly be the subject of a criminal investigation.

EXCHANGE-TRADED FUNDS

An Exchange-Traded Fund (ETF) is an investment that tracks an index, a commodity or a group of assets much like an index fund, but trades like a stock. ETFs are ***PASSIVELY-MANAGED***. ETFs represent shares of ownership of a *unit investment trust* (UIT). A UIT is a company that holds portfolios of stocks, bonds, currencies or commodities. Popular families of ETFs include:

- SPDRs
- VIPERs
- iShares
- PowerShares

ETFs have become very popular recently because they generally do not come with the same annual expenses like mutual funds. In fact, since they trade like stocks, the only commission you pay will be for the cost of the trade. However, it is important to note that some ETFs are *leveraged.* Being a leveraged ETF indicates that they are borrowing money to buy more investments. To illustrate this concept, let's look at a real-life example.

A few years ago my wife and I decided to purchase an investment property. Since we did not have the cash at the time to afford the down payment, we took cash, or equity, out of our home. We did this by refinancing our home loan, also known as refinancing our mortgage. Taking equity from our home resulted in a higher mortgage balance, which is certainly a risky thing to do. However, we used that cash to buy another asset; the investment property. We now own two homes, one which we rent out, and one that we live in. To summarize, we leveraged the equity in our home to buy the investment property. We subsequently increased our risk, but furthered our chances of potentially higher gains. Although this is not exactly the same as purchasing leveraged ETFs, the basic concept is similar. For beginning investors, I highly recommend staying away from these types of exchanged-traded funds.

As you can see, there are many factors to consider when investing in mutual funds and ETFs. While there are numerous advantages of mutual funds, their costs can erode some of your gains. Understanding the specifics of these types of investments can help you make informed decisions about which types of funds and ETFs will help you grow your investments over the long-term. Even if this chapter has left you feeling like mutual funds and ETFs are not the type of investments that you would explore, there is a very good chance you will not have that choice. Most employer retirement plans only allow you to invest in mutual funds and therefore, you will be forced to choose appropriate funds that meet your goals and risk tolerance. In the next chapter you will learn about other types of investments that are not as common as stocks, bonds, mutual funds, and ETFs.

"When I begin to invest, I'm going to start with mutual funds. They are the simplest way for a teenager to grow his or her money with less risk."

Sara Elwell, Ithaca College

CHAPTER SEVEN

WHAT ARE ALTERNATIVE INVESTMENTS?

In the last few chapters, we discussed the basic investments most people will purchase to meet their financial goals. However, there are many other types of investments that are available to investors. You may or may not invest in one or more of the following alternative investments in your lifetime, but it is beneficial to become familiar with them in case you decide otherwise. I actually contemplated leaving this chapter out of the book because most of us will never purchase alternative investments for a variety of reasons. If you would like to keep the information that you are absorbing right now at a basic level, I suggest you skip this chapter and revisit it at a later time.

In this chapter we will learn about various alternative investments and discuss their levels of risk while determining if their unique traits will have a place within our investment portfolios. There are too many types of these kinds of investments to cover in one book so we will talk about the ones that are the most important to understand, including:

- Closed-End Funds
- Hedge Funds
- Options
- Treasury Inflation-Protected Securities (TIPS)
- Futures
- Real Estate Investment Trusts (REITs)

CLOSED-END FUNDS

A closed-end fund is an investment fund that issues a ***FIXED*** number of shares in an actively-managed portfolio of securities. The shares are traded in the market just like stocks, but because closed-end funds represent a portfolio of securities they are very similar to a mutual fund. Highlights of closed-end funds include:

- They focus on one region or industry.
- They invest in stocks, bonds and other securities to gain diversification.
- There are several hundred closed-end funds traded on U.S. stock markets.
- Fixed interest payments are taxed at the same rate as the investor's income tax rate.
- Some closed-end funds are highly leveraged.

HEDGE FUNDS

A hedge fund has some similarities to a mutual fund. However, the investment strategies available to hedge funds and the types of investment positions they can take can be very complicated.

The general/limited partnership model is the most common structure for the investment funds that make up a hedge fund. In this type of legal company, the general partner assumes responsibility for the operations of the fund, while limited partners can make investments into the partnership and are liable only for the amounts they invested.

Understanding the objectives of the hedge fund is important to understand when deciding to invest in one of these alternative investments:

- Hedge funds seek to maximize returns by using aggressive strategies such as selling short, derivatives, and currency investing.
- They have **<u>MUCH</u>** higher fees than mutual funds they can be as much as 20% or more!!
- They are open to a limited number of investors, who usually must have a net worth of at least $1 million.
- Investments in hedge funds are *illiquid* as they often require investors to keep their money in the fund for at least one or more years.
- As of this writing, hedge funds are **<u>NOT</u>** fully regulated by the Securities and Exchange Commission (SEC).

The SEC is the governing body of the United States securities (or investments) industry that was created by Congress to regulate the securities industry and protect investors.

One of the most common measures of performance for a hedge fund is the *Sharpe Ratio*:

Sharpe Ratio = (Expected Portfolio Return – Risk-Free Rate)/ Portfolio Standard Deviation

- Expected portfolio return is the average return of the portfolio.
- The risk-free rate is the shortest dated U.S. Treasury Bill.
- *Standard deviation* is a statistical measurement that looks at historical volatility. The more spread apart the data, the higher the volatility.
- The higher the ratio, the higher the **RISK-ADJUSTED** return.

Risk-adjusted return is another way of looking at how much an investor made on an investment or investment portfolio. It takes into consideration the risk of the investments and adjusts the returns accordingly. If an investor takes on a great deal of risk, he or she should expect to see a greater return. Risk-adjusted return takes that additional risk into consideration.

Let's take a look at an example of how we can use the Sharpe Ratio:

Consider the following 2 hedge-fund managers:

- Manager A generates an average return of 18% in 2012.
- Manager A's portfolio has a standard deviation of 10%.
- Manager B generates an average return of 15% in 2012.
- Manager B's portfolio has a standard deviation of 6%.
- The risk-free rate of a U.S. Treasury Bill is currently 3%.

Use the Sharpe Ratio to calculate the risk-adjusted returns of the 2 hedge funds. Which manager was able to generate a higher return on a risk-adjusted basis?

Manager A:

Sharpe Ratio = (Expected Portfolio Return - Risk Free Rate)/ Standard Deviation
Sharpe Ratio = (18 - 3)/10
Sharpe Ratio = 15/10
Sharpe Ratio = **1.50**

Manager B:

Sharpe Ratio = (Expected Portfolio Return - Risk Free Rate)/ Standard Deviation
Sharpe Ratio = (15 - 3)/6
Sharpe Ratio = 12/6
Sharpe Ratio = **2.00**

In this case, Manager B had a higher return on a risk-adjusted basis.

OPTIONS INVESTING

Before we dive into options, I would like to make it clear that these types of investments are only for people who have a clear understanding of the different types of strategies that can be used to try to earn money. Although options can be quite complicated, it is important to attain the basic knowledge of how they work. Furthermore, if you mention options to your parents or even other investors, they may react in a very negative manner. They may say things like, "options are way too risky" or "options are only for investors who have millions of dollars". Of course they may never have heard of an option.

The point I am trying to make is that it is good to keep an open mind on ALL types of investments, including options. The truth of the matter is that options can be as risky as you want them to be or they could be more conservative that owning a stock. It all depends on the options strategy you are employing. The strategies we cover below are the most basic options strategies. There are many other more sophisticated methods when investing in options that may interest you, but this book would be over 600 pages long if we discussed all of them! Remember, never, I repeat, NEVER invest in options unless you have learned enough about them AND practiced trading them for at least one year. A good site to look at to practice trading options is www.cboe.com. Okay, let's get started!

An *option* is a legal contract that gives the buyer of the option the ***right***, but not the obligation, to buy or sell an asset at a specific price on or before a certain date.

- The 2 main types of options are *Calls* and *Puts*.
- A Call option gives the owner the right, but not the obligation, to ***BUY*** a specified amount of an asset at a specified price within a specified time. The specified price is known as the *strike price*. The cost for the right to buy the asset is known as the *premium*. The *expiration date* is the future date, usually the third Friday of the month, in which the right to buy the asset expires.
- A Put option gives the owner the right, but not the obligation, to ***SELL*** a specified amount of an asset at a specified price within a specified time. The specified price is known as the *strike price*. The cost for the right to sell the asset is known as the *premium*. The *expiration date* is the future date, usually the third Friday of the month, in which the right to sell the asset expires.

BUYING A CALL OPTION EXAMPLE:

- On June 1st, the stock price of Ed's Juice Bar (EJB) is $38 per share.
- The premium (cost) is $2.25 for an August 40 Call, which indicates that the expiration is the third Friday of August and the strike price is $40.
- The total price of the contract is $2.25 x 100 = $225. ***(One contract equals 100 shares)***
- You predict EJB will trade much **HIGHER** in the next few months.
- In order to capitalize on the anticipated rise in the stock, you decide to **BUY** one of the above call options.

Stock Price	$38
Strike Price	$40
Premium (Cost)	$2.25
# Options	1
# Shares	100

Let's take a look at how this transaction would unfold........

Our *maximum loss* would only be $225 because if the stock never exceeds $40 by the August expiration date, we would not exercise our right to buy the stock. Therefore, the option would expire worthless and we would only lose our initial investment of $225. Remember that we paid $225 ($2.25 X 100) for this position because the premium was $2.25 per share and we bought the *right* to buy 100 shares.

Our *maximum gain* in this position would be unlimited because the stock, in theory, could rise continuously. We would definitely exercise our right prior to the August expiration date when the stock passes $40 per share. Once we exercise our right to buy the stock at $40 per share, we own the stock outright and become owners of the company. Our investment performance is now determined by the rise or fall of the stock.

The *break-even price* of the stock is the price at which we would not make any money or lose any money on the position. The break-even price in this case is $42.25, which is the strike price of $40 plus the premium of $2.25 (Strike Price + Premium). If we exercise our right to buy the stock we would have to pay $40 per share. We also paid $2.25 per share for the option. Therefore, we would not make any money on the position until the stock exceeded $42.25.

Table 7.1 below provides the initial 'buying a call option' investment on June 1st as well as some examples of our gains or losses based on specific prices of the stock. Notice how we only lost $225 at the expiration date since the price of the stock was not at or above $40 per share.

Table 7.1

BUY CALL	June 1st	July 10th	Expiration Date
STOCK PRICE	$38	$45	$34
TOTAL STOCK VALUE	$3,800	$4,500	$3,400
TOTAL PREMIUM PAID	$225	$225	$225
EXERCISE CALL?	NO	YES	NO
COST TO BUY STOCK	N/A	$4,000	N/A
GAIN/LOSS	($225)	$275	($225)

SELLING A CALL OPTION EXAMPLE:

- On June 1st, the stock price of Ed's Juice Bar (EJB) is $38.
- The premium (cost) is $2.25 for an August 40 Call, which indicates that the expiration is the third Friday of August and the strike price is $40.
- The total price of the contract is $2.25 x 100 = $225. ***(One contract equals 100 shares)***
- You predict EJB will trade much **LOWER** in the next few months.
- In order to capitalize on the anticipated fall in the stock, you decide to **SELL** one of the above call options.

Stock Price	$38
Strike Price	$40
Premium (Cost)	$2.25
# Options	1
# Shares	100

Let's take a look at how this transaction would unfold........

Our *maximum loss* would be unlimited because if we sell the call option, someone else bought the option on the other end of the trade and hence, bought the right to buy the stock at $40 per share. If the stock rises above $40 per share, the buyer of the option will exercise his or her right to buy the stock from us at $40 per share. In theory, the stock could rise continuously so we run the risk of having to buy the stock at a very high price in order to deliver the shares to the buyer of the call option. For example, let's say the stock rose to $200 per share before the expiration date and the buyer of the call option exercised his right to buy the stock. As the seller of the call, we would have to go out into the market and buy the shares at $200 each in order to deliver the shares to the buyer. Since the buyer only has to pay us $40 per share, we lose $160 per share ($40 - $200 = -$160)!! Selling calls in this case, also known as selling uncovered calls, is not a wise choice for the majority of investors since the risk greatly outweighs the benefits. Selling *covered calls* simply means that you already own the stock when you sell the call options. This is a much more conservative options strategy which would limit your losses.

Our *maximum gain* in this position would be $225 because as the seller of the call option, we received $225 in cash from the buyer. If the stock never reaches $40 per share by the expiration date, the buyer will never exercise the right to buy the stock. Therefore, the option expires worthless and we would make a profit of $225.

The *break-even price* of the stock is the price at which we would not make any money or lose any money on the position. The break-even price in this case is $42.25, which is the strike price of $40 plus the premium of $2.25 (Strike Price + Premium). If the buyer exercises the right to buy the stock, he or she would have to pay us $40 per share. If the price of the stock was $42.25 at the time the buyer exercised his right to buy, we would have to go out in the market and pay $42.25 per share and deliver the shares to the buyer. The buyer would only have to pay us the strike price of $40 per share. Although we would lose $2.25 per share on the transaction, we must realize that we also received $2.25 per share from the buyer for the right to buy the stock. Therefore, we really broke even. We would begin to lose money after the stock price exceeded $42.25 prior to the time the buyer exercised the right to buy.

Table 7.2 below provides the initial 'selling a call option' investment on June 1st as well as some examples of our gains or losses based on specific prices of the stock. Notice how we can only make a profit of $225 regardless of how much the stock price is below $40 per share.

Table 7.2

SELL CALL	June 1st	July 10th	Expiration Date
STOCK PRICE	$38	$50	$39
TOTAL STOCK VALUE	$3,800	$5,000	$3,900
TOTAL PREMIUM *RECEIVED*	$225	$225	$225
BUYER EXERCISES CALL?	NO	YES	NO
BUYER COST TO BUY STOCK	N/A	$4,000	N/A
SELLER COST TO BUY STOCK	N/A	$5,000	N/A
GAIN/LOSS	$225	($775)	$225

BUYING A PUT OPTION EXAMPLE:

- On June 1st, the stock price of Ed's Juice Bar (EJB) is $38.
- The premium (cost) is $2.50 for an August 35 Put, which indicates that the expiration is the third Friday of August and the strike price is $35
- The total cost of the contract is $2.50 x 100 = $250. ***(One contract equals 100 shares)***
- You predict EJB will trade much **LOWER** in the next few months.
- In order to capitalize on the anticipated fall in the stock, you decide to **BUY** one of the above put options.

Stock Price	$38
Strike Price	$35
Premium (Cost)	$2.50
# Options	1
# Shares	100

Let's take a look at how this transaction would unfold........

Remember that when buying a put option, we are buying the right to SELL the stock on or before the expiration date. Consequently, our *maximum loss* in the above scenario would be $250 because if the stock price never goes down to $35 or below before the August expiration date, we would not exercise our right to sell the stock. Therefore, the put option would expire worthless and we would only lose our initial investment of $250. Remember that we paid $250 ($2.50 X 100) for this position because the premium was $2.50 per share and we bought the *right* to sell 100 shares.

Our *maximum gain* in this position would be $3,250. We arrive at this maximum gain by first realizing that the stock could only decline to as little as $0 per share. In the unlikely event that this happens, we would be able to buy 100 shares of stock for virtually nothing and simultaneously exercise our right to sell the stock at the strike price of $35 per share. In theory, that would be a gain of $3,500 ($35 X 100 shares). However, we paid $250 for the right to sell 100 shares of the stock ($2.50 X 100 shares). Therefore, our maximum gain can only be $3,250 ($3,500 - $250).

The *break-even price* of the stock is the price at which we would not make any money or lose any money on the position. The break-even price in this case is $32.50, which is the strike price of $35 minus the premium of $2.50 (Strike Price - Premium). If we exercise our right to sell the stock we would receive $35 per share. However, we paid $2.50 per share for the put option. Therefore, we would not make any money on the position until the stock exceeded $32.50, our break-even price.

Table 7.3 provides the initial 'buying a put option' investment on June 1st as well as some examples of our gains or losses based on specific prices of the stock. Notice how our profit increases as the price of the stock falls farther away from the break-even price of $32.50.

Table 7.3

BUY PUT	June 1st	July 10th	Expiration Date
STOCK PRICE	$38	$50	$20
TOTAL STOCK VALUE	$3,800	$3,000	$2,000
TOTAL PREMIUM *PAID*	$250	$250	$250
EXERCISE PUT?	NO	YES	YES
COST TO BUY STOCK	N/A	$3,000	$2,000
TOTAL SALE OF STOCK	N/A	$3,500	$3,500
GAIN/LOSS	($250)	$250	$1,250

T.I.P.S. (TREASURY INFLATION-PROTECTED SECURITIES)

United States Treasury inflation-protected securities (TIPS) are fixed-income investments that provide a hedge (or protection) against inflation risk. They are AAA rated bonds that provide us with what is called a *real rate of return.* The real rate of return of an investment is simply the rate of return of our investment minus the inflation rate. For example, if our mutual fund rose 8% in the year, but inflation that year was 5%, we really only made 3%. TIPS help shield our investment from this risk by providing the following:

- Protection against the value of TIPS by adjusting the value upward based on the inflation rate
- Providing interest payments that will increase when TIPS prices rise

You can buy TIPS through the U.S. Treasury or you can buy a mutual fund that consists of a variety of TIPS.

FUTURES INVESTING

Futures are contracts on commodities, currencies, and stock market indexes that you buy or sell. When investing in futures you are trying to predict the prices of assets at some point in the future (no pun intended). When a futures investor exercises the right to buy an asset at a specific price, the investor on the other side of the contract is obligated to deliver the goods. This could be oil, currencies, orange juice, pork bellies, and other assets. For example, someone buying one October Orange Juice contract at $4 a pound is obligated to accept delivery of 100 pounds of orange juice during the month of October at $4 a pound. If you are a seller of the contract, you are obligated to deliver the orange juice to the buyer. For another example of futures investing, ask yourself the following question: Why would an airline decide to buy futures contracts in oil? To help you with this question it is useful to look at Southwest Airlines, one of the few consistently profitable airlines in the United States. Southwest Airlines bought futures contracts in oil many years ago when oil was cheap to hedge future rises in oil. It turns out, as we all well know, that oil prices did rise significantly to record levels. Since Southwest Airlines acquired futures contracts at cheap prices they did not have to pay the astronomical prices for jet fuel that most airlines did. This, of course, translated into much lower operating costs for the company since jet fuel is the 2nd largest cost for airlines. By the way, the largest cost for the majority of companies is employees.

Various Types of Commodities Include:

Cocoa	Lumber
Coffee	Natural Gas
Copper	Oats
Corn	Orange Juice
Cotton	Platinum

Crude Oil	Pork Bellies
Feeder Cattle	Rice
Gold	Silver
Heating Oil	Soybeans
Live Cattle	Sugar

REITS (REAL ESTATE INVESTMENT TRUSTS)

A real estate investment trust (REIT) is a real estate company that offers common shares to investors. In this way, a REIT is similar to a stock, which represents ownership in a company. However, a REIT has two interesting features:

- Its main business is managing groups of income-producing real-estate properties
- It is required to distribute most of its profits as dividends to shareholders

To qualify as a REIT with the IRS, a real estate company must agree to pay at least 90% of its taxable profit to investors in the form of dividends. When a company is a REIT, it is not required to pay corporate income tax. A regular corporation makes a profit and pays corporate taxes. The company then decides what to do with their net profit. They can reinvest their profits, pay out some of the profits to shareholders in the form of dividends, or even keep some of their profits in cash. A REIT simply distributes all or most of its profits to shareholders which allows it to be exempt from most taxes.

Now that your mind is completely overwhelmed with the above information you can finally breathe a sigh of relief and be proud that you made it through without throwing the book in your basement for the next ten years! If I may, I'd like to suggest that you read through this chapter again to become clearer on some of the subject matter. Furthermore, you could always come back to it if and when you decide to invest your money in some of these alternative investments. In the meantime, consider yourself a more knowledgeable investor and be willing to take the necessary steps to learn the specifics of these investments if and when necessary. As a reader of the book, you can decide for yourself if alternative investments will have a place in your portfolio. However, please do not purchase any alternative investments without gaining a full understanding of the risks involved. Managing a simulated portfolio in order to practice for a year or two is a great way to avoid costly mistakes and gain valuable experience.

"Alternative investments can sometimes be a safer way to invest because they can offer a form of insurance against declining prices, but only if you know what you're doing – do not overestimate your financial knowledge."

-Tyler Bausinger, Villanova University

CHAPTER EIGHT

TYPES OF INVESTMENT ACCOUNTS

So far you have learned about many investment topics including types of investments. But where do you 'hold' these investments? In other words, if you buy a stock, bond, or mutual fund, where does it go? How do you access your investments if you need to sell them? These questions lead us to discuss the various types of investment accounts available to you as a consumer as well as an investor. Therefore, we are going to shift gears and talk about the advantages and disadvantages of various accounts designed for investors including:

- Standard Brokerage Account (Cash Account)
- Qualified Plans (including the popular 401k plan)
- SEP Plan
- Traditional IRA
- Roth IRA
- 529 College Savings Plan

- Education Savings Account (ESA)
- Margin Account

By no means is the list above the only types of investment accounts. There are many others that you may discover throughout your life. However, these accounts are certainly the most common that you will likely encounter in your investing career.

STANDARD BROKERAGE ACCOUNT

You're 18 years old and just graduated from high school. You only have $1,000 in your savings account and you are currently unemployed. However, after reading the stimulating information in 'The Early Investor', you have decided to invest your money! You talk to your parents about opening up an investment account and they give you the phone number for their financial advisor. Timidly, you make the phone call and proceed to talk to the financial advisor about investing your money. He explains to you that you need to open a brokerage account and make a cash deposit before you can actually purchase an investment. Later that day you visit his office, fill out and sign all the necessary paperwork, and hand him a check for $1,000 that will be deposited in your new investment account. Finally, he recommends that you purchase a balanced mutual fund with your money. Feeling overwhelmed with the entire process, you nod in agreement and realize that you would have agreed to any investment the financial advisor recommended.

In the scenario above, you opened up a standard brokerage account, also known as a cash account. This is the most basic type of investment account that is available to you. You open the account, deposit cash, and buy investments. Once you buy an investment, you can usually track the investment online. You will also receive account statements either online or through the mail. If your investment pays dividends, interest, or capital gains you will receive these earnings as cash that will be credited to your account. Of course, what do you think would be the smart thing to do with the earnings? Hopefully you realize the smart thing to do would be to reinvest any earnings into more shares of your investment. Once again, your earnings can be reinvested automatically if you choose to do so.

QUALIFIED PLANS (INCLUDING 401K PLANS)

We are now going to explore investment accounts that are specifically designed to help us save for retirement. This is where the fun begins because there are many advantages to these types of accounts. Some might seem too good to be true, but we will see that the advantages are real and highly beneficial to investors.

A qualified plan is a retirement account established by the employer for the benefit of the employee. These plans are required to adhere to ERISA standards set by federal law. ERISA stands for the Employee Retirement Income Security Act and is the law which private industries must follow in order to protect their employees. A qualified plan allows the employer to claim a tax deduction for contributing to the plan. Employees who make contributions make them on a *pre-tax basis* and their investment earnings grow *tax-deferred.* Contributing to a qualified plan simply means putting money into it from the money you make at your job. We will see an example of contributing on a pre-tax basis shortly. We will also discuss what tax-deferred means when investing within a qualified plan.

There are 2 types of qualified plans:

1. *Defined Benefit*
2. *Defined Contribution*

A defined benefit plan is a qualified plan where the employer makes contributions to the plan on behalf of the employee. In many cases, the employee will also be required to contribute a portion of his job earnings to the defined benefit plan. The contributions are deposited in a large pool of money and invested in various assets on behalf of members of the plan. One of the great features of a defined benefit plan is that the retirement benefits are guaranteed; hence the term defined benefit plan. This means that upon retirement the employee will receive guaranteed income for the rest of his or her life based on a formula. The formula is unique to each employer, but usually is composed of factors such as the age of the employee at retirement, the number of years he or she worked for the employer, and how much money the employee earned in certain years. The best example of a defined benefit plan is called a *pension plan.* The following bullet points summarize the main advantages of a defined benefit plan:

- The employee receives guaranteed income for life after he or she retires
- The employee can easily determine what age he can comfortably retire
- The employee will not have to worry as much about retirement because he or she has a good idea of how much money they will be receive from their plan

There are also some disadvantages to defined benefit plans:

- Employees have no control over investment choices within the plan
- While receiving guaranteed income when you retire is certainly a good thing, it limits your flexibility relevant to how much income you need and how much of your income benefits you can control.

Regarding the second bullet point, your income benefits could completely end upon your death. That certainly sounds like a morbid statement, but it is an unfortunate reality. Defined benefit plans, unlike other retirement plans we will cover, only pay out income benefits for the life of the employee or the life of the employee and their significant other. While the income benefits can be customized, the fact of the matter is that the benefits end at some point in time. If you live a long, happy retirement it really will not matter as much because you had time to reap the rewards of the plan. However, if you or your significant other do not live long after you retire, most of the money that was due to you goes away. This is not the case with other types of qualified and retirement plans.

By the way, what occupations typically offer good pension plans? Well, there are many. However, the most common would be local, state, and federal government jobs as well as jobs in education. Specific examples would be teachers, police officers, firefighters, and politicians. Pension plans used to be quite common many years ago within private industry, but most companies have done away with them because they could not afford to take the risk of having to pay guaranteed benefits regardless of how the stock market performed.

A defined contribution plan is the polar opposite of a defined benefit plan. In a defined contribution plan, the employee makes contributions to the plan and decides which investments he will purchase. The employee usually can choose these investments from a short list of mutual funds. In a small percentage of defined contribution plans the investment choices are much more flexible, allowing employees to invest in other investments such as individual stocks and bonds as well as certificates of deposits. The best and by far the most common example of a defined contribution plan is the 401k plan; therefore, we will concentrate on this specific type of plan. Most large corporations only offer a 401k plan to its employees. Consequently, your parents may very well have a 401k plan. When you begin working at your first significant job it is very likely you will be able to open a 401k plan through your employer. There are numerous advantages of a 401k plan including:

- Employee contributions are made on a pre-tax basis
- Many employers provide ***matching contributions*** to the plan on behalf of the employee
- Earnings on your investments are tax-deferred

The following is an example of contributing on a *pre-tax* basis:

Assume you earn $50,000 per year and pay 20% in income taxes. If you contribute $6,000 of that to your 401k, you won't have to pay tax on the $6,000! (See figure 8.1) Notice the significant difference in the amount of taxes you are paying when you choose to NOT take advantage of contributing to a 401k plan. Another way of looking at it is to realize that you are essentially making $1,200 just for contributing to the plan! In this case you are making a 20% return on your money because that is how much you do not have to pay in income taxes. This is because we reduced our taxable income by contributing $6,000 to our 401k plan. Ask yourself this question; can you find an investment that returns 20% to you instantly? I don't think so! And now we have $6,000 that can be invested in various mutual funds that will provide us with earnings and will likely rise in value over the long-term. Furthermore, any earnings from dividends, interest, and capital gains are tax-deferred. This means that you will not have to pay any taxes as your investments grow in value.

Table 8.1

CONTRIBUTE TO 401k		DO NOT CONTRIBUTE TO 401k	
Gross Salary	$50,000	Gross Salary	$50,000
401k Contributions	$6,000	401k Contributions	$0
Taxable Income	$44,000	Taxable Income	$50,000
Income Tax Rate	20%	Income Tax Rate	20%
Income Tax Paid	$8,800	Income Tax Paid	$10,000

We have mentioned contributing to a 401k plan several times already. How does this actually happen? Well, your contributions simply come out of your paycheck automatically, again on a pre-tax basis. The following example gives you an idea of the process of making contributions:

Patty earns $60,000 a year working for Microsoft as a computer programmer. She is paid twice a month. She contributes 13% of her salary to her 401k plan. How much, in dollars, does she contribute from each paycheck to her 401k plan?

Monthly Contributions to 401k= (Salary * % Contribution)/ number of pay periods
Monthly Contributions to 401k= ($60,000 * 13%)/24
Monthly Contributions to 401k= $325 each paycheck

You can see that $325 will come out automatically from Patty's pay check and she will benefit instantly from saving money on her income taxes. The $325 will also be automatically invested into more shares of her chosen investments. Patty can also manage her 401k plan online by changing her investment choices at any time. There are limits to how much you can contribute to a 401k plan. The **maximum** annual contribution to a 401k plan can be found on the irs.gov website.

DISTRIBUTIONS FROM A 401K PLAN

Distributions are simply defined as the removal of assets from a retirement account. In other words, it is when you withdrawal money from your account. The significance of a distribution is the fact that you have to pay taxes on the amount you withdrawal. The amount you are taxed is based on your federal income tax bracket. Recall that in a 401k plan you are not taxed on your contributions and you are not taxed on your investment earnings. Unfortunately, the government is going to tax you somewhere in any investment, and in most retirement plans it is when you withdrawal money from them. There are many rules that the Internal Revenue Service has created regarding distributions from retirement plans including:

- In general, distributions from a 401k plan must occur after age 59 ½.
- In general, distributions that occur before 59 ½ will be charged a 10% early distribution penalty.
- There are some exceptions to the 10% penalty rule
- The account owner must begin *required minimum distributions (RMDs)* the year he or she reaches age 70 ½.

The reason why you will be penalized 10% is because the government wants to create an incentive for you to save for your retirement years. However, you will not be penalized if you take a distribution before age 59 ½ for the following reasons:

- Upon and after the death of the account owner
- If the account owner becomes disabled
- If the account owner is at least 55 and has left his employer
- For certain medical expenses
- For higher education expenses
- For a down payment on a 1st home

There are other exceptions to the 10% penalty rule, but the list above covers the most common ones.

When the account owner of a retirement plan reaches age 70 ½, he or she is required to take a minimum distribution (RMD) based on a calculation that determines the amount. The reason why you are required to take a minimum distribution is that the government needs you to pay taxes to generate revenue so they can fund many federal programs.

Take a look at the following example to determine how much in taxes you will pay when taking a distribution from a 401k:

Jake, age 63, takes a $7,000 distribution from his 401k plan. His federal income tax rate is 25%. How much will he be taxed on the distribution?

Taxes on 401k Distributions= Distribution X Federal Income Tax Rate
Taxes on 401k Distributions= $7,000 X 25%
Taxes on 401k Distributions= $1,750

You can see that Jake has to pay quite a bit of money in taxes upon the distribution of his $7,000. Remember though that his contributions and earnings were not taxed at all.

EMPLOYER MATCHING

If you thought it couldn't get any better, wait until you read this next section! We will now spend some time learning about employer matching within a 401k plan. Matching is a type of contribution an employer *chooses* to make to an employee's retirement plan.

For example:

- You earn an annual salary of $50,000.
- You contribute $6,000 for the year to your 401k plan.
- Your employer matches up to 50% of the first 6% you contribute from your salary.

How much in dollars will the employer contribute to your 401k plan on your behalf?

Employer Matching Contribution = **Salary X 6% X % Matched**
Employer Matching Contribution = $50,000 X 6% X 50%
Employer Matching Contribution = $3,000 X 50%
Employer Matching Contribution = $1,500 in FREE MONEY!

Table 8.2 shows the huge benefit of employer matching. Once again, just for deciding to contribute to a 401k plan, you are reaping instant rewards; in this case free money! This is not a scam or a too good to be true story. This is reality and also one of the reasons I have a hard time understanding why some employees do not take advantage of their employer-offered 401k plan. If you do not contribute, you do not get the employer match. Why wouldn't anyone do this?! Look at the results in figure 8.2 in another way. Just for contributing $6,000 to the plan, you are receiving $1,500 in matching contributions which is a 25% instant return on your investment! ($1,500 divided by $6,000) And once again, you can invest this money in various mutual funds that will provide you with earnings and will likely rise in value over the long-term. Additionally, if you take into consideration the $1,200 you saved (or made) in taxes, you had a 45% instant return on your investment! ($2,700 divided by $6,000) Hopefully you are as excited about this valuable information as I am.

Table 8.2

CONTRIBUTE TO 401k		DO NOT CONTRIBUTE TO 401k	
Gross Salary	$50,000	**Gross Salary**	$50,000
401k Contributions	$6,000	**401k Contributions**	$0
Employer Match	$1,500	**Employer Match**	$0
Total Contributions	$7,500	**Total Contributions**	$0
$1,500 in FREE MONEY that you can invest!!			

VESTING

As you can see, employer matching is one of the greatest benefits of contributing to a 401k plan. There is one very important factor, however, when discussing matching contributions. Employees only have the right to claim the matching contributions after working a specific length of time for the employer. In other words, any matching contributions the employer makes on behalf of the employee will not be available to the employee unless they are *vested. Vesting* is the process by which the employee earns a right to benefits funded by employer matching contributions. For example, if you decide to leave your current employer after working there for two years and your employer matching is valued at $10,000, you might only be entitled to take 40% of that money with you. That translates into $4,000 and is much less than the $10,000 of free money you received and invested. If you worked there for three full years before leaving you would likely be entitled to 60%, or $6,000, of the money. After five years you would be fully vested in your 401k plan, which means that any past or future matching contributions will be fully vested and you are entitled to take 100% of that money upon leaving the company. Employers use vesting as an incentive for the employee to stay with the company. Hiring and training new employees cost companies a great deal of money so it is in their best interest to retain existing employees. Below are a couple of key points about matching contributions:

- Employees are always 100% vested in their own contributions.
- Employees are usually 100% vested in employer contributions after 3 or more years, but typically 5 years.

Let's take a look at a detailed example..............

Bob is 40% vested in his 401k plan. The employer's contribution represents $10,500 of the total value of the plan. His contributions represent $50,000 of the total value of the plan. What is the total VESTED value of his 401k?

Solution:

Vested Value of 401(k) = (% Vested x Value of Employer Contributions) + Value of Employee Contributions
Vested Value of 401(k) = (40% x $10,500) + $50,000
Vested Value of 401(k) = $4,200 + $50,000
Vested Value of 401(k) = $54,200

You can see that it pays (literally!) to remain at your current employer until you are fully vested. It is also important to understand that if you are considering leaving your company for another job you need to know how much you will lose in matching contributions if you have been there less than five years. This should be a factor in your decision-making process if you are faced with this scenario.

ESOP (EMPLOYEE STOCK OWNERSHIP PLAN)

An Employee Stock Ownership Plan (ESOP) is a defined contribution plan by which the investments are in the employer's stock. This type of defined contribution also comes with unique benefits. One benefit is that you can purchase your company's stock at a discount, usually around 15%. If the price of the stock is at $40 per share at the time you purchase it, you will only have to pay $34 per share (See Table 8.3). However, you cannot simultaneously sell the stock and cash in on your 15% profit. Much like matching contributions, you can only sell the stock after a specific period of time. ESOPs usually have their own vesting schedule independent from an employer matching contribution schedule. Many employers implement an Employee Stock Ownership Plan to create an incentive for employees to perform well and help make the company more profitable. If employees have a vested interest (again, no pun intended!) in the company by owning its stock, they will likely work harder and exceed expectations.

Table 8.3

Price of Employer Stock	% Discount for Employees	Discounted Stock Price
$40	15%	$34

In your opinion, is it a good idea to participate in an ESOP rather than a 401k plan? That is an interesting question which leads us back to the topic of diversification. Since we are only invested in our company's stock in an ESOP, our risk is significantly greater. This, as always, leads me to another story of how diversification is an important tool to manage risk.

A friend of mine has worked for the same company for over 25 years and accumulated a large number of shares of the company stock through an ESOP. In 2007 the company stock he acquired had a market value of approximately $800,000. We had numerous conversations over the years where I pleaded with him to diversify his retirement portfolio by selling some of the company stock. His reaction was similar to other conversations I have with clients who think their investments will never go down significantly. He would explain to me that his company stock has been going up for years and that he has made a lot of money on it by not selling any of it. I think you know how this story ends. In 2008 the stock went down about 95% in a very short period of time and the company almost went bankrupt! When the storm had passed, my friend's $800,000 of company stock was only worth about $40,000! Not only did he lose most of the value of the stock, he lost almost all of the money he had saved for college expenses for his kids. The moral of this story is to never, ever take your investment profits for granted. In other words, do not be greedy!

One very important point I would like to make about an ESOP is that you can choose to contribute to both an ESOP and a 401k plan at the same time. This could be a good strategy to use that allows you to take advantage of the discount on your company stock as well as being well diversified in your overall retirement portfolio. Just make sure that you are not investing too much in your ESOP so that your risk is not inherently greater than you can handle.

SEP (SIMPLIFIED EMPLOYEE PENSION)

We can see how it is highly beneficial to take advantage of your employer's qualified plan. But what if you work for a smaller company that does not offer a defined benefit or defined contribution plan? How about if you are self-employed, which happens to be a growing trend in the United States, and you cannot access a qualified plan? Well, you are in luck, my friend! A Simplified Employee Pension, or SEP, will allow you to participate in tax-advantaged retirement planning. A SEP is a retirement plan established by employers, including self-employed individuals. Many smaller companies that usually have fewer than 100 employees will offer a SEP plan. Employers make tax-deductible contributions on behalf of all its employees. A SEP plan is NOT considered a qualified plan, but there are some similarities:

- Contributions to a SEP are tax-deductible for the company as well as for a self-employed individual; therefore, contributions ultimately are not taxed
- Investment earnings grow on a tax-deferred basis

There are also some unique advantages to a SEP when compared to a qualified plan:

- SEPs are easy to administer
- Your investment choices are very flexible

- You can potentially contribute much more to a SEP when compared to a qualified plan
- As an employee, you do not have to contribute anything to your SEP because your employer makes all the contributions on your behalf

Unlike qualified plans, SEPs are easy to set up and maintain and thus, have lower costs associated with the plan. Since qualified plans are for larger companies and must follow ERISA guidelines, there are greater costs that employers and employees must pay. This is not the case with SEPs. I have a client who owns his own business and has about five employees working under him. When I opened up a SEP for him and his employees, I simply logged onto the site I use when opening accounts, filled out all of the pertinent information, printed out copies and mailed them to the client. The client then signs all of the forms, mails them back to me, and begins to make contributions to the plan. It is that simple!

Recall that the majority of 401k plans only allow you to invest in a handful of mutual funds. One of the greatest features of a SEP is that you can invest in a wide variety of investment choices. This includes mutual funds, individual stocks and bonds, certificate of deposits, real estate, and even gold and silver coins.

Another great feature of a SEP is that you can contribute much more to it when compared to a 401k plan. Back in 2015, an employer could contribute up to 25% of the employee's compensation, providing the contribution did not exceed $53,000. (Check the irs.gov website for updated SEP contribution limits for current years.) The following example illustrates how SEP contributions are determined for a self-employed individual:

Matt owns his own business and does not have any employees working for him. He is planning on paying himself $210,000 this year in salary. If he opens up a SEP plan, what is the **maximum** contribution he can make to the plan this year?

Maximum Annual Contribution to SEP= The lesser of $53,000 or (Salary X 25%)
Maximum Annual Contribution to SEP= $210,000 X 25%
Maximum Annual Contribution to SEP= $210,000 X 25% = $52,500
Maximum Annual Contribution to SEP= $52,500

You can see that Matt can only contribute a maximum of $52,500 to his SEP in 2015. However, that is much more than the maximum annual contribution to a 401k plan. Of course, not many of us will make $210,000 in a year. Let's take a look at another example:

Monica owns her own business and does not have any employees working for her. She is planning on paying herself $44,000 this year in salary. If she opens up a SEP plan, what is the **maximum** contribution she can make to the plan in 2015?

Maximum Annual Contribution to SEP= The lesser of $53,000 or (Salary X 25%)
Maximum Annual Contribution to SEP= $44,000 X 25%
Maximum Annual Contribution to SEP= $44,000 X 25% = $11,000
Maximum Annual Contribution to SEP= $11,000

In the above example, Monica can only contribute a maximum of $11,000 given her relatively small income level this year. Understand, however, that Monica might not be sure she is paying herself $44,000. If her business has a bad year she may pay herself much less than $44,000. This situation is much different when you are an employee of a company where you know how much you are going to make in a given year. When you are self-employed or an owner of a small company, it is difficult to forecast your earnings. This is why SEP plan contributions usually occur towards the end of the year when small company owners and self-employed individuals have a better idea of how much they will be allowed to contribute.

There is one 'risk' when you are an employee of a small company that offers a SEP. Unlike 401k plans where you decide when and how much to contribute to your plan, employees with a SEP have no say on contribution amounts or when contributions will occur. The reason is that contributions are at the sole discretion of the employer, which means that in any given year employers can decide not to contribute anything to the plan. If they feel the company did not have a good year or they actually lost money, they may contribute nothing to your SEP plan. If the company has several years of negative earnings you might not see anything contributed to your SEP for quite some time. However, if the owner or owners of the company owner decides to contribute to the plan, he or she has to contribute the same percentage to ALL employees. They cannot decide to contribute only to their plan or only some of their employees.

You can see how SEPs can be a great type of retirement plan for smaller companies and self-employed individuals. I come across many electricians, plumbers, contractors, consultants, and others who do not realize they can establish and contribute to a SEP plan even though they work for themselves. There are many young people today that will eventually become self-employed and will benefit from a SEP. It is a huge advantage to know that this type of retirement plan is available to you if you are one of them.

DISTRIBUTIONS FROM A SEP

Distribution rules for a SEP are very similar to those of a 401k plan:

- In general, distributions from a SEP must occur after age 59 ½.
- In general, distributions that occur before 59 ½ will be charged a 10% early distribution penalty.

- There are some exceptions to the 10% penalty rule
- The account owner must begin *required minimum distributions (RMDs)* the year he or she reaches age 70 ½.

The same 401k plan exceptions to the 10% penalty for distributions prior to 59 ½ apply to a SEP.

Take a look at the following example to determine how much in taxes you will pay when taking a distribution from a SEP:

Max, age 57, takes a $10,000 distribution from his SEP. His federal income tax rate is 15%. How much will he be taxed on the distribution?

Taxes on SEP Distributions= Distribution X Federal Income Tax Rate
Taxes on SEP Distributions= $10,000 X (15% + 10% Tax Penalty)
Taxes on SEP Distributions= $2,500

You can see that Max has to pay a 10% tax penalty in addition to his regular federal income taxes because he took a distribution prior to age 59 ½.

TRADITIONAL IRA

Individual Retirement Accounts (IRAs) were created by Congress to help supplement retirement income for individuals and their households. Technically speaking, IRA stands for Individual Retirement Arrangement, but there are few people who refer to it as that. The first type of IRA we will learn about is the Traditional IRA. The following are some of the highlights of a Traditional IRA:

- A Traditional IRA is a retirement account where contributions can be tax-deductible and earnings grow on a tax-deferred basis.

- Money in a Traditional IRA is not taxed until it is withdrawn.

Just like qualified plans and SEPs, you may not have to pay any tax on contributions and your investment earnings grow on a tax-deferred basis. Notice how you MAY not have to pay taxes on your contributions. If you make too much money you will not be allowed to deduct your contributions from your income. This essentially translates into the fact that you would have to pay taxes on your contributions. Don't worry though! As a young investor you will likely not have to worry about that until you begin to make a significant amount of money. It is also important to realize that a Traditional IRA has nothing to do with your employer. It is completely separate from any type of qualified plan or SEP. In order to establish and contribute to a Traditional IRA you must follow the criteria below:

- Any individual, regardless of age, who has *taxable compensation* for the year and will not reach age 70 ½ by the end of the year.
- Any individual, regardless of age, who has *self-employment income* for the year and will not reach age 70 ½ by the end of the year.

Notice the term 'taxable compensation' in the first bullet point above. Taxable compensation is comprised of any of the following:

- Salary
- Wages
- Commissions
- Bonuses

Now let's look at what is NOT considered taxable compensation:

- Mowing your neighbor's lawn and getting paid in cash
- Babysitting and getting paid in cash

- Any job you perform where you get paid in cash

Basically you need to receive a paycheck for it to be considered taxable compensation. If you work for a company, you are more than likely receiving taxable compensation. Once you start receiving a paycheck you can open up a Traditional IRA. How do we actually contribute to one once it is opened?

- Make a contribution to your IRA account.
- Make a contribution to your spouse's IRA account.
- Transfers
- Rollover contributions

The **maximum** annual contribution to a Traditional IRA can also be found on the irs.gov website. To make a contribution to your Traditional IRA, you simply deposit an amount no greater than your total gross compensation (compensation before deductions) for the year. For example, if your gross pay for the year was $3,000 you can only contribute up to $3,000. Keep in mind, however, you can only contribute up to the maximum annual amount for the given year.

A nice feature of a Traditional IRA is that you can establish and contribute to one on behalf of your spouse even if he or she does not have any taxable compensation for the year. This allows you to essentially double the amount of money you can invest for retirement. Remember that an IRA is for an individual so your spouse's Traditional IRA will be a completely separate account under his or her name.

You can contribute to your IRA in the form of a check which you mail to the investment firm where you opened the IRA or you can wire the money from your bank account. You can also transfer money automatically each month from your savings or checking account to your Traditional IRA account. Once again this is a form of dollar-cost averaging.

If you already have a Traditional IRA, you can rollover the assets into a new one that you recently established. Rolling over assets from an existing Traditional IRA to a new one has nothing to do with the maximum contribution limit. Hypothetically, you could have $1,000,000 in an existing Traditional IRA and roll it over to a new one.

Another advantage to a Traditional IRA is that you can invest in a wide variety of investment choices, just like in a SEP. This includes mutual funds, individual stocks and bonds, certificate of deposits, real estate, and gold and silver coins.

DISTRIBUTIONS FROM A TRADITIONAL IRA

Distribution rules for a Traditional IRA are very similar to those of a 401k plan and a SEP:

- In general, distributions from a Traditional IRA must occur after age 59 ½.
- In general, distributions that occur before 59 ½ will be charged a 10% early distribution penalty.
- There are some exceptions to the 10% penalty rule
- The account owner must begin *required minimum distributions (RMDs)* the year he or she reaches age 70 ½.

The same 401k plan and SEP exceptions to the 10% penalty for distributions prior to 59 ½ apply to a Traditional IRA. Take a look at the following example to determine how much in taxes you will pay when taking a distribution from a Traditional IRA:

Jack, age 58, takes a $6,000 distribution from his Traditional IRA for paying his daughter's college tuition. His federal income tax rate is 35%. How much will he be taxed on the distribution?

Taxes on Traditional IRA Distributions= Distribution X Federal Income Tax Rate
Taxes on Traditional IRA Distributions= $6,000 X 35%
Taxes on Traditional IRA Distributions= $2,100

Jack does NOT have to pay a 10% tax penalty because he took a withdrawal from his Traditional IRA to pay for his daughter's college tuition, which is one of the exceptions to the 10% early distribution we discussed previously.

ROTH IRA

The retirement plans we have discussed all have identical tax advantages. The contributions and investment earnings are not taxed, but when taking a distribution, income taxes must be paid. If you had a choice, would you rather be taxed on your distributions from your retirement plan or on your contributions? More specifically, given your age, when would you prefer to be taxed in your retirement plans? This is a very interesting question that could shed some light about which type of investment account would be appropriate for teenagers and young adults. Think about the answer in terms of your situation as a young investor. Whether you are a teenager with a part time job or starting your first significant job out of college, you are likely in a very low tax bracket. In other words, you are paying very little right now in federal income taxes. If you have a job you will notice that there are federal income taxes being taken out of your paycheck. The amount taken out will likely get much higher as you begin to earn a higher amount throughout your career. Therefore, the choice of when you would want to be taxed in a retirement plan should be easy. At this point in your life wouldn't you want to be taxed now at a low rate rather than be taxed later when your federal income tax rate will almost surely be higher? Absolutely! The answer to this question leads us to the celebrated Roth IRA. Some highlights of a Roth IRA are as follows:

- A Roth IRA is a retirement account where contributions are NEVER tax-deductible and earnings grow on a *tax-free* basis
- Assets in the Roth IRA are *NOT* taxed when they are withdrawn

First, let's take a look at the significant advantage of a Roth IRA over the other retirement plans we have discussed thus far. We can see in Table 8.4 that Roth IRA contributions are never tax-deductible. The obvious result is that you are paying taxes on your contributions. Second, notice that investment earnings grow on a tax-free basis and NOT on a tax-deferred basis. What this means is that since you already paid taxes on your contributions you do not have to pay taxes when you take distributions. Hence, the term 'tax-free' growth of investment earnings. Tax-deferred growth means that you are not paying taxes *until* you take a distribution. (See Table 8.4 for a Traditional IRA vs. Roth IRA comparison) In other words, you are delaying, or deferring the payment of taxes. In a Roth IRA you can take all qualified distributions completely tax-free as long as you are at least 59 ½ years old. Imagine retiring and not having to worry about taxes on your income you take from your retirement plan! The Roth IRA is one of the best choices for many people for this reason. And it is even better when you are younger.

Table 8.4

TRADITIONAL IRA	ROTH IRA
Contributions May Be Tax-Deductible	Contributions Made With After-Tax Dollars
Your Investment Earnings Grow Tax-Deferred	Your Investment Earnings Grow Tax-Free
You Pay Income Taxes On Distributions	You Do Not Pay Income Taxes On Distributions

I'd like to clear up a common misconception about contributing to a Roth IRA. In the table above we can see that contributions in a Roth IRA are made with *after-tax* dollars. This is just another way of saying that we are paying taxes on our contributions. For example, assume you had a part-time job working at McDonald's and you earned a gross income of $4,000 in that year. Let's assume you decided to contribute the full $4,000 that year to your Roth IRA. You do not have to pay federal income taxes after you contribute because you already paid them. The federal tax you paid came out of your paychecks throughout the year. Therefore, your $4,000 that you contributed to your Roth IRA is considered after-tax contributions. In order to establish and contribute to a Roth IRA you must follow the criteria below:

- Any individual, regardless of age, who has *taxable compensation* for the year
- Any individual, regardless of age, who has *self-employment income* for the year
- To make a contribution, the individual must have a gross income that is less than a certain amount

DISTRIBUTIONS FROM A ROTH IRA

Distribution rules for a Roth IRA are similar in some ways when compared to a 401k plan, SEP and a Traditional IRA:

- In general, distributions from a Roth IRA must occur after age 59 ½.
- In general, distributions that occur before 59 ½ will be charged a 10% early distribution penalty.
- There are some exceptions to the 10% penalty rule
- However, Roth IRA account owners do NOT have to take *required minimum distributions (RMDs)* the year he or she reaches age 70 ½.

The same 401k plan and SEP exceptions to the 10% penalty for distributions prior to 59 ½ apply to a Traditional IRA. However, as a Roth IRA account owner, you are not required to take minimum distributions. Now you may be asking yourself, "why wouldn't I want to take withdrawals from my Roth IRA especially since I do not have to pay any taxes if I am over the age of 59 ½"? This is a difficult question to answer because it is not black or white. If we think in terms of where we are in our lives, we might be able to shed some light on this intriguing question. Teenagers and young adults have very different goals and ambitions and are generally only responsible for their well-being. People who are retired have a distinctive mindset. It is quite possible that if you are retired you will not need to take distributions from your Roth IRA. Maybe you have a pension plan, Traditional IRA, standard brokerage account, or even a savings account that adequately replaces your income. In this case there is no need to access your Roth IRA for income. Furthermore, you could plan to leave something to your family upon your death. A Roth IRA would be ideal for your heirs since the tax-free growth will still be intact upon the transfer of the account. I realize it sounds slightly morbid to discuss the transfer of your retirement accounts upon your death, but it is an unfortunate reality that we eventually become older and pass on. Now that I have brought the overall mood of the book from exciting to sobering, let's take a look at the following example to determine how much in taxes you will pay when taking a distribution from a Roth IRA:

Lisa, age 68, takes a $3,000 distribution from her Roth IRA. Her federal income tax rate is 25%. How much will she be taxed on the distribution? The answer is zero! She will not be taxed at all since the distribution was from a Roth IRA and she is over 59 ½.

Much like the Traditional IRA, you can establish and contribute to a Roth IRA on behalf of your spouse even if he or she does not have any taxable compensation for the year. You can contribute to your Roth IRA in the form of a check, which you mail to the investment firm where you opened it, or you can wire the money in from your bank account. You can also transfer money automatically each month from your savings or checking account to your Roth IRA account. If you already have a Roth IRA, you can rollover the assets into a new one that you recently established. Just like the Traditional IRA, you can invest in a wide variety of investment choices. This includes mutual funds, individual stocks and bonds, certificate of deposits, real estate, and gold and silver coins.

529 COLLEGE SAVINGS PLANS

The next account we will discuss is a 529 College Savings Plan. You may have heard of it through your peers, your parents, or from an advertisement. Your parents or grandparents may have established one on your behalf to help pay for your college expenses. In any case, learning about 529 College Savings Plans is important to managing your overall financial future. When you get married and have a family (and you probably will), one of the largest expenses you will need to plan for is college. It is no secret that college expenses have risen astronomically over the years and have outpaced inflation for much of the time. Failure to plan for education expenses can severely affect your retirement plan. I have had many new clients who had their hands tied when trying save for retirement because they were burdened by the high cost of college. They waited until the last minute to worry about it and had to take multiple loans out or dip into their retirement savings. This is certainly a recipe for financial disaster. A 529 College Savings Plan can help you invest for the future of your children and has many advantages including, but not limited to:

- Tax benefits
- Control by the account owner, not the child
- Low maintenance
- Flexibility
- Ability to make large contributions

The greatest advantage of a 529 plan is that it works much like a Roth IRA in the sense of its tax advantages. Table 8.5 compares the tax advantages of a Roth IRA and a 529 plan. You can see that they are identical except that qualified distributions have a different meaning for a 529 plan. Qualified distributions from a 529 plan include:

- Tuition & fees
- Room and board
- Books
- Technology required for classes
- Expenses for a special-needs student

Table 8.5

529 COLLEGE SAVINGS PLAN	ROTH IRA
Contributions Made With After-Tax Dollars	Contributions Made With After-Tax Dollars
Your Investment Earnings Grow Tax-Free	Your Investment Earnings Grow Tax-Free
You Do Not Pay Income Taxes On Qualified Distributions	You Do Not Pay Income Taxes On Qualified Distributions

A unique feature of a 529 plan is that the account owner maintains control of the money. The account owner is usually a parent or grandparent, but can be any family member. The account owner names a beneficiary of the account which is usually the child who will be attending college in the future. The owner controls many aspects of the plan including:

- Contributions made to the plan
- Investment choices
- Change in beneficiary designation
- Distributions from the plan

The age of the beneficiary does not matter. The account owner controls every aspect of the plan and can change beneficiaries at any time. Changing beneficiaries can certainly be a positive. If the child decides not to attend college, you can easily change the beneficiary to another one of your children or even a niece or nephew. From the beneficiary's point of view, it can be a negative if you need to access the money from the 529 plan and the owner decides to change beneficiaries. If this occurs, you are out of luck. Of course most account owners would never do that unless something detrimental happened to your relationship with them. The point I am trying to make is that you never know what can happen to the 529 plan if someone else controls it.

EDUCATION SAVINGS ACCOUNTS (ESAS)

Education Savings Accounts, or ESAs, are another choice for saving for college. ESAs are similar in some ways to 529 plans, but also have some distinct differences. Some similarities between ESAs and 529s are:

- Both have earnings that grow on a tax-free basis
- Both are not taxed when taking qualified distributions
- Both will be taxed AND penalized 10% on non-qualified distributions
- Both allow you to change the beneficiary of the account at any time

The following is a list of differences between ESAs and 529s:

- ESA assets can be used for private elementary or high school expenses as well as for college
- The maximum annual contribution to an ESA can be found on the irs.gov website

- Allowable investments within an ESA are flexible including individual stocks, bonds, CDs, mutual funds, and other choices.
- In general, the assets in an ESA must be used for educational expenses before the beneficiary reaches age 30.

Although there are limitations on how much you can contribute to an Educational Savings Account, you can use the money for private schooling prior to college. This is a unique feature of ESAs and is a huge advantage over 529s if you are planning on sending your children to private schools.

MARGIN ACCOUNT

A margin account is a standard brokerage account with borrowing features. A margin account is something you add on to your brokerage account that allows you to borrow money from the brokerage firm. The brokerage lends the customer cash with which to purchase additional investments. A margin account allows an investor to buy investments with money that he/she does not have, by borrowing the money from the broker. The Federal Reserve limits margin borrowing to at most 50% of the amount invested. Some brokerages have even stricter requirements, especially for volatile stocks. Investors open margin accounts to take advantage of an opportunity to leverage their investments. Brokerages charge an interest rate on margin loans. To summarize, buying on margin is simply borrowing money from a broker to purchase additional stock and other investments. Some highlights of a margin account are:

- Margin trading allows you to buy more stock than you would be able to normally.
- Margin is an example of *leverage:* The use of various financial instruments or borrowed capital to increase the potential return of an investment.

- You can borrow up to 50% of the purchase price of a stock.

To better understand how a margin account works, let's look at the following examples.

Example #1: You deposit $10,000 in your margin account. This means you have $20,000 worth of buying power because you deposited cash for 50% of that amount. Then, if you buy $5,000 worth of stock, you still have $15,000 in buying power remaining. You have enough cash to cover this transaction and have not tapped into your margin. You start borrowing the money only when you buy investments worth more than $10,000 because that is the amount of cash you deposited, also known as your *equity*.

Before we discuss the dreaded *margin call*, we must understand a restriction called the *maintenance margin*. The maintenance margin is the minimum account balance you must maintain. Maintenance margin is usually set at 25% of the value of your account. If your account balance falls below the minimum, your broker will force you to deposit more funds or sell stock to pay down your loan. When this happens, it's known as a margin call.

From example #1 above, let's take a look at what could happen in a specific situation:

- You purchase $20,000 worth of stocks by borrowing $10,000 from your brokerage and paying $10,000 yourself. How much equity do you have to start?

    ✓ **<u>Answer:</u> $10,000 (the amount you paid in)**

- The value of the stocks falls to $15,000. How much equity do you have now?

    ✓ **<u>Answer:</u> $5,000 ($15,000 - $10,000)**

- Assuming a maintenance requirement of 25%, how much SHOULD you have in equity in your account?

    ✓ **Answer:** **$3,750 (25% of $15,000)**

- Given this situation, will you receive a margin call?

    ✓ **Answer:** **No!** Your $5,000 in equity is greater than the $3,750 in equity required

Example #2:

- You purchase $40,000 worth of stocks by borrowing $20,000 from your brokerage and paying $20,000 yourself. How much equity do you have to start?

    ✓ **Answer:** **$20,000 (the amount you paid in)**

- The value of the stocks falls to $26,000. How much equity do you have now?

    ✓ **Answer:** **$6,000 ($26,000 - $20,000)**

- Assuming a maintenance requirement of 25%, how much SHOULD you have in equity in your account?

    ✓ **Answer:** **$6,500 (25% of $26,000)**

- Given this situation, will you receive a margin call?

  ✓ **<u>Answer:</u> Yes! Your $6,000 in equity is less than the $6,500 in equity required**

- How much will you be required to deposit in cash OR how much in stock do you have to sell to cover the margin call?

  ✓ **<u>Answer:</u> $500 ($6,500 - $6,000)**

As a young investor it may be difficult to get approved to open a margin account because you likely do not have a large amount of cash to deposit into an account. Even if you did have a sizable amount your brokerage might not approve it since you do not have much experience investing. The fact that they may not approve a margin account for you is actually a good thing. As you can see, margin accounts can be very risky because you are buying investments on borrowed money and you have to pay your brokerage back with interest. From the examples above we can see that this works very well when your investments go up in value, but can be a disaster if they go down. As a financial advisor I rarely recommend my clients buy investments on margin for obvious reasons. The majority of investors do not need to take on the additional risk. When the stock market crashed in 2001 and 2008, investors that owned stocks on margin lost thousands of dollars, even millions of dollars in some cases, due to their leveraged investments and large margin calls. Some investors lost everything! You may be asking yourself, "Why then would he write about margin accounts?!" The short answer is that, once again, you need to acquire the knowledge to make informed decisions in your investment portfolio. Buying on margin could be something you want to explore at some point in your life, but be aware of the risks and challenges they present.

We have covered all of the major types of investment accounts and now should have a good grasp on each of their advantages and disadvantages. As a young investor, choosing which account is right for you can help you maximize your returns on your investments and bring you closer to your short and long-term goals.

"As I move on to college, I have recognized the need to start saving and investing for my future. Opening a Roth IRA account is the smartest way to do this since my investments will be able to grow on a tax-free basis."

-Samantha Piotti, Boston University

CHAPTER NINE

MANAGING YOUR INVESTMENT PORTFOLIO

You are investing in your 401k plan, contribute to your Roth IRA each year, and own investments within a standard (taxable) brokerage account. Although only 26 years old, you are on your way to financial independence, following the golden rules of investing that you learned from 'The Early Investor' book you read as a teenager. Having a great start on investing for your future, you realize that many of your friends and co-workers seem stressed about their finances. Some of them have strained relationships with their significant others due to poor financial decisions and the lack of savings and retirement money. But not you! Your life, although challenging, is sailing smoothly because you do not have to worry as much about investing for retirement since you have already established a plan. You were also smart along the way, establishing an emergency fund and staying out of major debt. You have lived a frugal life thus far, but have still enjoyed the many opportunities the world can provide. After feeling good about the great start you had in your investment portfolio, you wonder how you can improve your returns while managing your risk. You already have an appropriate asset allocation and have properly diversified your investments in each account. However, in the past three years, the stock market went up an average of 15% per year. Consequently, your asset allocation has significantly changed since you opened up your investment accounts. Let's review some of the specifics of the above scenario.

- Your appropriate asset allocation based on your goals and risk tolerance is 70% stocks, 25% bonds, and 5% cash
- You are investing in your 401k plan and receive your employer's full matching contribution
- You contribute the maximum to your Roth IRA each year
- You have a standard brokerage account where you invest some of your discretionary income
- You have already established an emergency fund
- You have no serious debt concerns; only a mortgage on your home
- You have read 'The Early Investor'!

Because the stock market has risen and bond prices have fallen over the past few years, your asset allocation has changed. Your allocation is now 85% stocks, 10% bonds, and 5% cash. In order to get back to your proper allocation percentages you need to *rebalance* your portfolio. Rebalancing your portfolio is a portfolio management technique that can enhance your investment returns by selling assets that have appreciated in value and buying assets that have gone down in value. In other words, it means that you are buying low and selling high. You may have heard that expression before and thought to yourself that it sounds easy to do. Contrary to popular belief, it is very difficult to follow the buy low, sell high concept. Imagine how difficult it is for me to advise a client to sell some of their stocks that have gone **up** in value. Furthermore, it can also be hard to tell a client they should buy bonds because they have gone **down** in value. However, that is exactly what should be done to the portfolio in this situation. Stocks do not go up every year, nor do bonds go down every year. If that were the case, investing would be easy, and everyone would be a successful investor because they would know which direction a particular asset class would be heading.

There is one word that sums up why it is difficult to buy low and sell high: emotion. Emotion is the reason why most investors find it a challenge to beat the returns of the general market. For example, you may have participated in a stock market game in school where you can invest fictitious money into stocks of your choice. Although the game can be exciting, it is not real money. You may win, but you also may finish in last place. Even if you come in last place, it does not affect your financial goals because it isn't real. Conversely, the first time you invest real money, your anxiety levels will increase to levels unknown to mankind! Consider the following scenario:

You have $2,000 saved up and you decide to invest the money in a stock priced at $20 per share. After your account is open and you have deposited cash into the account, you go on the Internet and open up the trading window of your brokerage. Eager to make a trade, you nervously fill out the pertinent information including the stock ticker symbol, the number of shares you want to buy, and the 'buy' selection in the drop-down menu. When completed you hang the mouse arrow over the 'Submit Trade' button and appear concerned whether you are being smart or being reckless. You still hesitate to click the button as you intensely observe the stock price, hoping it will go down just a little bit more before you buy it. Finally, you hit 'Submit Trade' and realize you are officially a real investor. Of course, you have a variety of emotions coming over you all at once including excitement, anxiety, hopefulness, and curiosity.

What do you think most people will do after submitting their first trade? I remember my first trade vividly and I can share with you exactly what I did after clicking submit. The moment I clicked the submit button I started watching the stock to see if the price was going up or down. That is what most new investors will do because it is the first time they used real money to buy stocks. This is when our emotions get the best of us.

Imagine watching as the 100 shares of stock you bought for $20 per share starts trending down right after you purchased it. After an hour, the stock price drops to $19 per share. Your $2,000 is now worth only $1,900. You have already lost $100 and you wonder why you did this in the first place. As the stock continues to trend down, albeit a slower pace, you decide to cut your losses and sell the stock before risking losing more of your money.

What you actually did was lock in your losses when you decided to sell. Your emotions got the best of you. Instead of walking away and allowing the stock to settle down, you watched the price movement with a keen eye and sold out of emotion. Most new investors will do the same thing after buying their first stock. Assuming you invested in a quality company that has a long history of earnings, the smart thing to do would have been to hold the stock for the long-term. However, that is easier said than done. Fear becomes prevalent. The fear of losing money consumes you and causes you to make hasty decisions.

Let's take a look at what would likely happen if you changed the above scenario so that the stock you bought went *up* in value after buying it. Assume your $20 stock doubled in price to $40 per share in just a two week period. Now, before we proceed, I need to add a quick note here about this situation. Any stock that doubles in price in just a two week period is most likely a company that carries significant risk. You should not be investing in a stock like that unless you are well aware that you could conceivably lose all or most of your money just as fast as you made money. Anyway, getting back to the scenario, your total value in the stock is now $4,000! You knew it was a very risky investment, yet you were lucky. That's right, you were lucky! Please do not think to yourself that it is easy to find a stock that doubles in price within a few weeks or even a few months. What would most people do in this situation? The following list is a common outcome of the above scenario:

1. You watch the stock closely and decide to wait until it goes up just a little bit more before you sell.
2. After the stock price trickles down to $38 per share, you tell yourself you will sell as soon as it goes back up to $40.

3. The stock price goes down to $30 per share after a few weeks, but you decide to hold it anyway because you are "absolutely sure" it will go back up.

4. After watching the stock trend all the way down to $10 per share after a couple of months you decide to not even sell it because you have lost enough already so "what's the point".

5. Ten years later you still own the stock dubbed by you "a piece of junk", but you are emotionally attached to it so you keep it in your portfolio.

Why do we believe that we can determine where a stock price will move on a daily basis? If it was that easy we would all be millionaires, or even billionaires.

Analyzing the outcome above, I can tell you that it is a euphoric experience when your investment rises in value that quickly. Taking the emotion out of the decision-making process would have caused you to do the smart thing, which would have been to sell and lock in your profits.

SYSTEMATIC REBALANCING

Systematic rebalancing is the regular process of shifting money from over-performing assets to under-performing assets. This is one of the simplest ways to manage your portfolio and to limit your risk. Systematic rebalancing should be done at least once a year and more often in some cases. For example, if the stock market drops substantially over a three month period, it may be a good time to shift some of your over-performing investments into stocks. I know that may sound like a risky thing to do at the time, but that is an example of buying low and selling high. Let's take a look at a more specific example.

Assuming your appropriate asset allocation is 50% stocks and 50% bonds, you invest $25,000 in stocks and $25,000 in bonds. Over the next year, your stocks are up 40% and your bonds are down 30%. Your stocks are now valued at 35,000 and your bonds are valued at $17,500. Your asset allocation becomes approximately 67% stocks and 33% bonds. At this point you should certainly rebalance your portfolio back to 50% stocks and 50% bonds to maintain your appropriate allocation. The following year stocks are down 30%, but bonds are up 40%. Looking at table 9.1 shows us the difference in your portfolio values after the second year when rebalancing versus doing nothing. It should be quite obvious that you should rebalance again after year two since your proper asset allocation is no longer in sync. One of the most important concepts to understand is that the main goal of rebalancing is to minimize risk in your portfolio. Although higher returns are possible through systematic rebalancing, they are NOT guaranteed.

Table 9.1

REBALANCE PORTFOLIO (End of Year 2)		DO NOTHING (End of Year 2)	
Stocks	$18,375	Stocks	$24,500
Bonds	$36,750	Bonds	$24,500
Total	$55,125	Total	$49,000
% Return	10.25%	% Return	-2.00%

Think about the previous example in terms of being a consumer. If you want to buy a new big screen TV, are you willing to pay the full price or would you wait until it is on sale? The savvy consumer will most certainly wait until it goes on sale. I rarely buy items that are not on sale even if I have to wait a little while. The same concept applies to stocks and bonds and other investments. In 2011, the price of gold rose to an all-time high. I was not willing to buy gold at the time because I felt that the price grew too quickly. While no one has a crystal ball, it is usually wise to invest your money after an asset has declined in price for a while.

Although it is practically impossible to buy stocks at their absolute low point, it is obviously beneficial to buy them when they have dropped in value. Most young investors will "follow the herd" and sell when the market has gone down a great deal. Conversely, they will buy stocks when the market has already increased dramatically. This is a recipe for a series of financial losses. Following the herd rarely yields acceptable returns on your investments.

THE PRICE TO EARNINGS (P/E) RATIO

There are many factors to look at when deciding what stock to buy for your portfolio. Some of the general questions I like to answer when analyzing companies include, but are not limited to, the following:

- Does the company have a long-term history of positive earnings?
- Does the company have a long-term history of positive earnings growth?
- Is the company a leader in its industry?
- Does the company pay a dividend?
- Has the company raised its dividend in most years?
- Do I understand the business that the company is in?

The questions above are certainly not the only ones you should ask when looking at stocks to buy. There are numerous data variables that can help us analyze companies such as the PEG Ratio, Return on Equity, Operating Margin, and the Debt Ratio. If you have an interest in analyzing stocks and other investments and you enjoy working with numbers, you may want to consider becoming an analyst. However, for the purpose of this book, we will concentrate on one of the first criteria I look at when choosing a stock; the Price to Earnings (P/E) Ratio.

The P/E Ratio is a basic calculation that takes the current price, or market value, of the stock and divides it by its earnings per share or EPS. For example, at the end of the trading day, ABC stock closed at a price of $36.95 per share. ABC announced earnings of $1.80 per share for the year. What will the P/E ratio be for ABC?

P/E Ratio=Market Value per Share/EPS
P/E Ratio=$36.95/$1.80
P/E Ratio=20.53

What does a P/E Ratio of 20.53 really mean? Well, to make this easier to understand, let's dissect the mathematics of the problem. If we wanted to make 20.53 into a fraction we would simply take the 20.53 and put it over the number 1. The number 20.53 would be the numerator and the number 1 would be the denominator. If we labeled the two numbers, the numerator of 20.53 would represent the price per share of the stock and the denominator of 1 would represent the EPS. This is fairly obvious because that is what the above equation tells us. Therefore, a stock with a P/E Ratio of 20.53 means that investors are willing to pay **$20.53** for every **$1** of earnings the company generates.

The P/E Ratio helps us determine if a stock is undervalued, overvalued, or fairly valued. The average P/E Ratio for stocks is usually lies somewhere within a range of 15-25. Companies that have high growth rates typically have a P/E towards the higher end of the range. Many technology companies fall into this category. Microsoft at one time had a P/E ratio over 100! The reason why it had a P/E ratio over 100 was because investors were expecting the company to grow its earnings exponentially even though it was not as well-known as it is today. If you were looking at its stock at that time, it would have appeared to be very expensive to buy. However, we all know what happened with Microsoft. Looking back, it was probably one of the best companies you could have invested in at the time. What would have happened to Microsoft stock if it did not grow at a feverish pace? The stock likely would have fallen enough in price so that the P/E ratio was more in line with historical values. The price would have adjusted according to its earnings per share.

What about stocks that have a very low P/E Ratio such as 6.50? Could this mean that the company is extremely undervalued and it is a really good time to buy the stock? That may be the case, but it could also mean that there is something fundamentally wrong with the company's business model or that their product or service is no longer in high demand. The main idea you should take away from this is that the P/E Ratio is only a starting point when analyzing stocks. There are many other variables to research such as the ones previously mentioned.

PROBLEMS WITH THE P/E RATIO

There are a few issues you should take in to consideration when looking at the P/E Ratios of companies. Have you heard of a company called Enron? Enron falls into the category of a company with severe accounting issues. For years the company reported strong earnings growth which was reflected positively in the stock price. Then one day the company fell from grace. The media reported that Enron was being investigated for accounting fraud. The result was one of the biggest accounting fraud cases in history because Enron was actually losing millions of dollars. The stock basically went down to zero and the company went bankrupt while investors and employees of the company lost much of their retirement savings. It does not matter how well you analyze a stock if the company is "cooking the books", as the saying goes.

The P/E ratio does not consider any substantial rise or fall in the rate of inflation. Extremely high or low inflation rates can have a significant effect on a company's bottom line because they will have to either raise or lower prices of their goods and services. Consequently, the demand for their product or service may also be affected.

Investors and stock analysts have different interpretations of the P/E ratio because of the number they use for the denominator in the formula. Some may look at what is called "forward-looking earnings" which means they are using what they *expect* the company to make in profits over the next four quarters or year. Others may use "backward-looking earnings" meaning they will use the trailing four quarters of earnings or the actual profits the company made over the last year. Many times it is difficult to find out which earnings are being used in the formula.

Portfolio management is an important aspect of investing that should not be overlooked. Taking just a small amount of time to evaluate how your portfolio is performing is critical to becoming a successful investor. More importantly, portfolio management will help you minimize risk and meet or exceed your financial goals by maximizing your potential returns of your investments.

"Most people assume that investing is based on pure luck: investors simply buying stocks and praying for their investments to grow. However, actively managing your portfolio by diversifying, hedging risk, and rebalancing turns the odds heavily in your favor."

-Tejas Shah, University of Maryland

CHAPTER TEN

CONCLUSION & WHERE TO BEGIN

Hopefully after reading this informative book you are getting yourself ready to become an investor. But where do you go to open up an investment account and how do you know which one is best for your situation? First of all, I need to make it very clear that you most likely do NOT need a full-service financial advisor right now. Financial advisors are usually needed only when you have a substantial amount of money to invest. They also provide advice on other areas of your financial life including liability management, wealth protection, and estate planning. These areas are not as important when you are young, but as you grow older you will need to add them to your overall financial picture. Furthermore, most accomplished financial advisors would prefer not to have someone as a client who is just starting out and has little to invest. It is not worth their time because they will not make any money from these types of clients. They concentrate more on clients who have hundreds of thousands of dollars or even millions of dollars to invest. Fear not, however, because you can get to that point if you invest wisely and become financially disciplined!

There are many choices you have to open up an investment account when you are young. The list below includes some of the options to choose from:

- Vanguard
- Fidelity
- Charles Schwab
- E*Trade
- Scottrade
- TD Ameritrade
- ING Direct

All of these investment companies offer standard brokerage accounts as well as retirement accounts. Remember, 401k plans are offered through your company and not directly through a broker. However, you can certainly open up a Traditional IRA or a Roth IRA at any of these firms.

Vanguard and Fidelity offer low-cost mutual funds and are two of the most well-known and trusted companies in the investment world. If you would like to start investing in mutual funds, Vanguard and Fidelity would be good choices as they have some of the most widely-held funds available to you. They also are known for their wide selection of index funds. Both have great websites (www.vanguard.com and www.fidelity.com) that provide education as well as contact information where you can speak to someone about opening an account.

Charles Schwab is an investment firm that has many branches around the country where you can visit and speak to someone about opening an account. They are considered a discount broker and offer other types of services that can help you begin to invest. Charles Schwab is a good choice if you prefer to invest in a variety of assets such as stocks, bonds, and mutual funds. Although they also have a very good website, it is a good idea to go to one of the branches instead since there is likely one in your area. Regardless, there website is www.schwab.com.

E*Trade (www.etrade.com), Scottrade (www.scottrade.com), TD Ameritrade (www.tdameritrade.com), and ING Direct (www.ingdirect.com) are reputable choices if you are comfortable opening an online investment account. You will never actually see a human being or be able to visit a physical location in most cases. However, they do have toll-free numbers you can call to speak to someone who can help you open an account and even put through an order to buy or sell an investment. You also need to be comfortable with sending them your money after you open the account. Like many other products you can buy online, trading stocks and other investments are usually much less expensive through these investment firms.

All of the companies that are listed above offer the ability to set up a dollar-cost averaging strategy. Vanguard in particular offers the ability to purchase most of their mutual funds as long as you can invest at least $50 a month. Some of the companies also offer a checking account that you can attach to your investment account.

WATCH OUT FOR HIDDEN FEES

Opening an investment account is much like opening a savings or checking account at your local bank. You need to have a clear understanding of any fees associated with the account. You also need to read the "fine print" when filling out the required forms and reading the literature they provide to you. Sometimes it is difficult to sort out what charges might apply to you in certain situations. Isn't it amazing how most of this information is given to you in really small print?! Below is a list of some of the possible hidden fees you might encounter:

- ✓ Fees for transferring assets in or out of an account
- ✓ Account maintenance fees

- ✓ Inactivity fees
- ✓ Fees for not maintaining a minimum balance
- ✓ Sales charges on certain investments such as mutual funds

One of the fees that typically can surprise you is the inactivity fee. Inactivity fees are especially prevalent in online trading accounts. While these accounts have low trading fees, placing no trades for an extended period of time can trigger enormous fees. Make sure you are fully aware of how and when inactivity fees may be charged to your account.

TYPES OF STOCK TRADES

You decide to open up an online trading account and deposit $2,000 into it. You place the information in the online trading window to purchase a stock. One of your selections you need to make is the type of trade you want to use. There are numerous types of stock trades you can choose from such as:

- Market order
- Limit order
- Stop order
- Stop Limit order
- All or None
- Good until cancelled (GTC) order
- Fill or Kill

A market order requires immediate execution of the buy or sell trade at the best available price. What exactly does it mean to execute a trade at the "best available price"? To help us understand what it means we need to discuss the process of a trade.

Let's say that you are interested in buying stock in ABC company and the stock has a *bid price* of $10.00 and an *ask price* of $10.05. The bid price is the **highest** price a buyer is willing to pay for the stock at that moment in time. Conversely, the ask price is the **lowest** price a seller is willing to accept for selling the stock. Therefore, the *spread* between the bid and ask price for ABC stock is five cents. If you place a market order to buy the stock you will buy it at a price of $10.05 because that is the ask price which is the best available price of the seller at that time.

A limit order is an order to buy or sell at a specific price. Using the numbers above, we can specify the price that we are willing to pay for the stock. We can put a buy limit at $10.00 per share for ABC stock. Or even $10.01, $10.02, $10.03, $10.04, and $10.05. We can also place a buy limit order at $9.00 per share if we wanted. None of these buy limits would execute if there wasn't a seller willing to sell the stock to you at your specific price. Furthermore, using the previous example, if we submitted a buy limit order at $10.00 per share and the bid rises to $10.05 and the ask to $10.10, our trade will not execute at all unless the bid and ask prices came back down. However, with a buy limit order, you are guaranteed that you will buy the stock at the price you stated or better.

You may be wondering why a few cents per share matters so much. The truth is it will not make much of a difference when investing a small amount of money. However, when you start investing tens of thousands of dollars after you become wealthy you will care a great deal. A few cents will make a significant difference when that time comes. Hopefully sooner than you think if you start investing now!

Sometimes you may be interested in investing in a company that does not trade too often. In this case a limit order is very helpful because you will not be susceptible to wide fluctuations in the price of the stock. Companies that have very low trading volumes have much wider spreads. For example, the bid on a low volume stock may be $10.00, but the ask may be $10.75. A market order to buy the stock would execute at $10.75! If you used a limit order, you could specify the price that you are willing to pay for it. If you specify the price at $10.25, you may or may not get it, but at least you will not be paying too much.

A sell limit is similar to a buy limit except that you specify the price at which you are willing to sell the stock. If a stock is trading at around $20.00 per share and you want to sell it at $22.50 per share, you can submit a sell limit order at $22.50. If the stock price rises to $22.50, your stock will automatically be sold at that price or higher.

A stop order is a market order that trades after a specified level is reached. For example, if you own a stock that trades at $50 per share, you can submit a stop order to sell it at $40 per share. The stop order will only execute if the stock price falls below $40 per share. This type of order can be a huge advantage for investors who are looking to limit their losses.

Conversely, a stop order can be used to guarantee profits. For example, if you buy a stock at $20 per share and it doubles to $40 per share, you can submit a stop order at $35 per share. If the stock price drops to $35 or below, your trade will turn into a market order and execute immediately at the best price available.

Can you think of a situation when a stop order will not work as planned? Think about when significantly bad news comes out about a company. Will bad news come out during the trading day? Absolutely not! Negative news will almost always come out *after* the market closes or early in the morning *before* the market opens. Using the example above, setting the stop price at $35 per share might not be favorable if the company announces terrible news when the market is closed. In this scenario, the price of the stock may initially open the next trading day at a price far below $35. Consequently, your stop order might execute at the significantly low price it opens at. If the stock begins trading at $15 per share, that is the approximate price you will receive after the trade executes.

A stop limit order is almost identical to a stop order except that it automatically converts into a limit order when the stop price is reached. In this case, your trade may or may not execute depending on the movement of the stock because it has to hit your specified price.

An All or None order is a stipulation you add to your buy or sell order that states that you want all of the shares that you requested to buy or sell. If your order cannot be filled entirely by the end of the trading day, the order will be cancelled. For example, if you submit an All or None order to buy 1,000 shares of a stock at $40 per share, the order will not be filled until the entire 1,000 shares can be bought at that price. When I was a young investor I found out the hard way about All or None orders. Many times I put an order in to buy stock only to find that the trade was only partially executed. I had to put an additional trade in the next day to obtain the other shares which led to more commissions I had to pay and sometimes higher stock prices. An All or None order prevents investors from having orders only partially filled before they expire.

A Good Until Cancelled (GTC) order is another stipulation you can add to an order that does not automatically cancel at the end of the trading day. The order will remain indefinitely until your trade executes or until you cancel it. It is important to note that some brokerage firms will cancel your order permanently after a specified period of time even though you added the GTC stipulation. In this case make sure you ask your broker how long a GTC order will last.

A Fill or Kill order is also a stipulation you can add to an order that requires immediate execution. If it cannot be filled immediately, it is cancelled. This order is useful if you are trading a large number of shares and you do not want the order sitting out there until all the requested shares are bought or sold.

Are you ready to be challenged on the types of trades you can use to help you achieve your goals and manage risk? Remember, your results will not be recorded so you have nothing to lose! You can find the answers on the following page.

STOCK TRADE QUESTIONS

1. Kyle wants to place an order with his broker for 20,000 shares of Google (GOOG). However, he wants to make sure the broker can fill the entire order. What type of order should he use?

2. Steve wants to place an order with his broker for 1,000 shares of Gemalto (GTO). However, the current price is $24.10. He only wants the trade to go through if it reaches $24.00. What type of order should he use?

3. Mike owns 5,000 shares of Orman (SUZ). He has made a ton of money on this company, but he may want to sell his shares because he doesn't want to lose what he has gained. The current price is $104.50, but he also thinks it might continue to go up. What type of order should he use to try to protect his gains?

4. Kim wants to place an order with her broker for 10,000 shares of Pfizer (PFE). However, she wants to make sure the broker can fill the entire order. What type of order should she use?

5. Frank wants to place an order with his broker for 5,000 shares of General Electric (GE). However, he wants to make sure he buys at a specific price. What type of order should he use?

6. Stan, so far, has made a big profit on his 15,000 shares of Verizon (VZ). VZ is currently at $50.00 per share. He paid

$20.00 per share when he bought the stock. He wants to place a trade that will allow him to sell the stock immediately at the best available price. What type of order should he use?

7. Molly is afraid of losing her profit she made on her 7,500 shares of Apple (AAPL). AAPL is currently at $500.00 per share. She paid $150.00 per share when she bought the stock. She wants to place a trade that will allow her to sell the stock automatically if it falls to $450.00 per share. What type of order should she use?

8. Rob wants to place an order with his broker for 5,000 shares of Waste Management (WM). WM is currently at $35.00 per share. However, he only wants to buy it if it goes down to $32.50 per share. If he places the order now, what type of order should he use?

9. Jack wants to place an order with his broker for 100,000 shares of Mcdonald's (MCD). However, he wants to make sure that all the shares can be bought. What type of order should he use?

10. Ed wants to place an order with his broker for 500 shares of Kraft (KFT). However, he wants immediate execution at the best available price. What type of order should he use?

ANSWERS TO STOCK TRADE QUESTIONS

1. All or None

2. Limit Order

3. Stop Order

4. All or None Order

5. Limit Order
6. Market Order
7. Stop Order
8. Limit Order
9. All or None Order
10. Market Order

I would like to share some final thoughts that will hopefully motivate you to begin investing for your future. As a teenager or young adult, time seems to be endless. And certainly you have a bright and exciting life ahead of you. However, Father Time does eventually catch up and rear its ugly head. Just ask your parents or your grandparents. It seems like yesterday that I was still in high school hanging out with my friends and thinking about the senior prom or leaving for college that summer. Investing was the farthest thing from my mind. As I look back to those memorable days, the only thing I would change would have been to open up an investment account to start preparing myself financially for my future. In those days few people educated my generation on the importance of investing early. You now have that knowledge and inspiration to do something that could greatly enhance your future. Be proud of your accomplishments, but be smart and be proactive. Be different from your peers and begin your quest for wealth and financial independence tomorrow. Good luck and I wish you the best on your exciting adventure through life!

"If you were to ask any long-term investor what they really wanted, they wouldn't say big houses or exotic cars, they would likely say more time. Nothing is more valuable when it comes to investing money than time. In the beginning, thirty cent returns may seem like a waste of time, but if you remain in the market long enough and keep reinvesting, eventually they become 100 dollar returns; and then 1,000 dollar returns. But reaching that point takes time."

-Spencer McCullough, Pennsylvania State University

CHAPTER ELEVEN

A SPECIAL CHAPTER FOR PARENTS

As a parent of three boys, I can say with utmost confidence that educating our children on investing is one of the most important gifts we can give them. While it is sometimes difficult to find time in our crazy schedules to teach our children about investing and other financial topics, the effort we make will be appreciated as they grow older.

Rather than inundate you with material more suited for a textbook or limited to only my opinion, I felt it would be more productive to interview a few other parents to learn from their experiences and to share their ideas on how to raise financially responsible children.

The first parent I would like to introduce is Michael Garry. Michael is a Certified Financial Planner, owns Yardley Wealth Management, L.L.C. in Bucks County, Pennsylvania, and is a frequent expert contributor to financial publications. He has been quoted in Money Magazine, Kiplinger's, BusinessWeek.com, CNNMoney.com, and Consumer Reports Money Advisor as well as being featured in the Wall Street Journal. Michael is the father of three girls. God bless him!! I asked Michael how he plans on teaching his girls about saving and investing. I also asked him to share his thoughts on how to raise financially independent children.

"It's definitely challenging. Our kids are bombarded daily with messages that they "need" all of these material things and they need them now. It's all about instant gratification. I try to counter that by trying to get my girls to focus on the big picture. They have a limited amount of income and need to decide how much they will save and invest, how much they will give to charity, and how much they will spend. Although the dollars are smaller and they don't have the same living expenses we adults have, many of the decisions are similar. If you spend it, you can't use it later for some other purpose. I hope that it makes them think twice about what they spend their money on so they just don't do it mindlessly.

I use our business and personal lives as examples. I talk about the mistakes I made when I was younger and how I wish I had saved more then and how if I did, my business would have been less risky to our family when I was starting it. Because of my business, our income is not static. So each calendar quarter my wife and I make decisions on how much to reinvest in the business, how much to save in our personal accounts, how much to save for the girls' educations, and how much to give to charity. Whatever is left is what we feel comfortable spending. I talk to my girls and tell them the real numbers and my thoughts behind doing things the way we do. I encourage them to ask questions and sometimes they ask really good ones!

I try to stress that they'll need to invest for themselves and in themselves, meaning they need to have cash savings and investments, (I prefer index mutual funds for investing), but they'll also need to make sure that they have money saved so they can get the training and education they need for whatever their chosen fields will be. Again using myself as an example, I go to two conferences every year where I spend a lot of time taking classes and learning how to make my business better for me and my clients. It's a big investment in time and money, but I think the return on the investment in education in my field is well worth it and I hope that lesson gets through to them."

The next parent I would like to introduce is Frank J. Mayo. Frank is a high school district curriculum coordinator, an educational consultant, and was the 2010 Pennsylvania Business Educator of the year. I asked Frank to reflect on his unique methods he uses to instill a sense of financial self-reliance within his students and his three children.

"I always tell my students to BE RESPONSIBLE. I want them to always be accountable for their actions. This holds very true for their personal money management principles as well. Young people need to rely on themselves and make rational decisions regarding their money. I preach to them that the only person that they can trust is themselves. They are the only one that can decide whether they can truly afford something or not. They should not let others influence their spending habits or decisions. Young adults need to think about the financial consequences and results of their actions and do what is in their own best interest. No one person is ever going to have a better understanding of what is best for you than yourself.

Another issue in fiscal responsibility with young adults is that they never bother to look at their receipt from a purchase, the bill from dinner, or even an invoice from an on-line purchase. They need to look at hidden fees, costs, or even items that they did not receive in the transaction. It is very unlikely that someone else is going to catch a mistake made on one of their transactions. There is a good chance that someone will be looking to capitalize on their lack of financial accountability and possibly take advantage of them. This is why they need to trust themselves and BE RESPONSIBLE."

Rich Oring is the president of New Century Financial Group, L.L.C. in Princeton, New Jersey and has written financial articles for local newspapers. He is the father of three boys.

"I'm a financial advisor and a father of three young boys ranging from the ages of three to nine. As a parent I wonder how I am going to teach the values of saving to my children. They are challenged each day with the newest toys and electronics coming to the markets.

How can I convince them to stop competing with their friends who have the coolest and newest gadgets to come out? My job is to try to show them and teach them that saving today will pay off in the future.

My wife and I allow our children to earn money by doing chores around the house. This can range from 25 cents to 5 dollars depending on the task. It is amazing to see how each child reacts to the opportunity for earning some money. My oldest will only do chores when he is within reach of purchasing something he wants. My middle child will do chores and save the money. The big difference is that my oldest will only do the chore to have gratification on buying something, but lacks the foresight on saving for the future. Whereas my middle child has no short term thoughts on how to spend his money and is happy to see it accumulate in his piggy bank.

So as a parent I have to approach each of the two children differently. I am trying to have my oldest become more disciplined on what he is buying. He had a tendency of wanting the first thing he can buy with his money. We discuss buying something now or waiting and saving more money to buy something which is better. This is getting easier since the cooler toys or electronics are now costing more than 5 dollars. He is saving for things which might take weeks or months to buy. I believe that this is a good step for saving.

My middle child is much easier to work with because he isn't always thinking on how to spend his money. Saving and watching it accumulate is more like a game for him. Hopefully this will continue as he gets older.

I understand that my children are much too young to learn about stocks and bonds. So the way I have been teaching my children about earning interest on their money is by having them open savings accounts at the bank. With the interest rate being so low, my wife and I secretly deposit a few dollars here and there so my kids get excited when they receive their bank statements. They find it amazing to see how their money can grow by just leaving it in the bank. As a parent I am happy when my kids fill their piggy banks and ask to go to the bank. We make a big deal about going. We usually go out first for pancakes and then head over to the bank on a Saturday morning. I would encourage this strategy for young investors."

Mike English serves as the President and CEO of the Missouri Council on Economic Education (MCEE) and is a Visiting Professor of Economics at the University of Missouri-Kansas City. He is the father of two sons.

"Although children react differently to attempts to teach them about money, I find that it is helpful to connect economics to their personal interests. Like many boys, my older son loves baseball and video games. There are some really good sports metaphors for investing--particularly Major League Baseball. When a team invests in a player, there is always risk involved. But by researching the player's statistics, potential, and upside, teams attempt to mitigate their risk. Small market teams have far less margin for error. Since we root for a small market team, I talk to my son about the human capital that our team is investing in at the minor league level. I have found that many video games offer teachable moments as well. Although kids might not recognize it, there are great incentives in various games to save and think strategically. By pausing the game and initiating a discussion about the economics at work in the game, my son either (a)appreciates what I'm trying to teach him, or (b)loses interest in the game (so I win either way!).

I struggle a bit to teach my sons to understand that investing is a long-term process. They are eager to make a quick profit, but the real key to investing is patience. Since I have opened 529 plans for both of my sons, I decided to be very transparent with them about the college savings accounts. I want them to understand that their parents make tradeoffs every single month. One of these tradeoffs is to give up some current consumption in favor of investing in their futures. I share the quarterly performance of these 529 plans with my sons. They get very excited to see their portfolios grow, which offers a very good opportunity to research stocks and mutual funds together.

While investing can be exciting, saving can be boring. Therefore, I try to encourage my boys to set short-term savings goals and help them find ways to earn money. If my son is saving up for something that costs $50, I will often provide some quick tasks for him to earn a few dollars. We then brainstorm together about ways to earn some money. These ideas have included selling books to a used bookstore, looking under couches and chairs for loose change, and setting up a lemonade stand. The closer my son gets to his goal, the more excited he becomes."

Dr. Donna Dunar is a former principal and is currently an Assistant Superintendent of Curriculum and Instruction for a Pennsylvania school district.

"As the mother of two boys, ages 13 and 11, I have tried to teach by life's example. When the boys were young, I gave them a modest allowance which they would save and sometimes spend on candy, toys and books. This was my way of teaching them the value of money. As I reflect, I realize that as they have become adolescents, I have not been giving them an allowance, and yet, they have not been asking for it.

As an educator, I have come to realize the importance of teaching kids not only to be "smart", but also to be "good". We want smart students who will know how to invest their own money and other people's money, i.e., we do not want kids to grow up like Bernie Madoff. Ethical decision-making is at the heart of success. Resiliency and empathy also need to be taught. I stress resiliency, empathy and ethical decision-making with my two sons. Responsibility, respect, citizenship are also important factors. So far, I am not disappointed. Intrinsic rewards are working for us.

My husband suffered a massive stroke in 2005. My sons are growing up seeing their father adjust from working a challenging job as a K-9 police officer to staying home. While this adjustment isn't easy, it enables me to work long days and nights in my role as an assistant superintendent of schools. My two sons have witnessed sacrifice, hard work and the importance of striving to do one's best. I have emphasized with them the importance of taking the most challenging courses in school. This can provide the avenue to a good career and a means to provide for oneself and a family. Whether it is on the lacrosse field, running track, or in the classroom, my sons strive to do their best. As a mother, teacher, principal and assistant superintendent, "Reach for the stars!" has long been my mantra."

Robert Leonard works for a large 'blue-chip' corporation and has experience in a variety of fields including sales, marketing, and risk management. He is the father of a teenage daughter.

"When I first tried to teach my daughter about saving, she was quite young – too young. I was idealistic – I was going to do it the right way: start early and find every opportunity to reinforce the message for the next 20 years. The $2 allowance she was getting at the time split into two, $1 to save and the other to spend, didn't add up to much very quickly. And the pennies in interest she would earn from the bank was not much of an incentive, either. We hadn't talked to her yet about the cost burden of holiday gifting and she was too young to have a consumption function of her own, so in retrospect I probably should have expected that "what on earth for?" look she gave me. How do I make this real for her?

Our 2nd approach was the same one that resonated with me as a young boy. To prime the pump, my wife & I socked away a couple dollars into an account for her each week. By the time the holidays rolled around the account had grown to an eye-popping level (for her, anyway). We had her attention. Instead of starting at ground zero and forcing her to make that tough decision with her allowance every week, we demonstrated the value of automating the saving process. It was easy; all she had to do was make the decision one time and forget about it. She has been doing it that way with her own money ever since.

Now 14, with a bigger savings account and a typical teenager's wants and needs, it's difficult enough to get her to focus on school work and chores. The right time for a conversation about investing will be when I can make it real for her. Life-lessons resonate with her now in ways they couldn't when she was younger and she is beginning to understand the tradeoffs that come with every decision she makes. And with that real life experience in weighing those tradeoffs, she'll have the footing she needs for the discussion about investing and I'll have a way to make it real for her. But for now, thank goodness we don't need to worry about whether she's saving."

The above opinions should give you some useful ideas on how to instill financial discipline within your children. I have discussed this topic with many parents in my adult lifetime and have heard numerous ways to accomplish this goal including, but not limited to:

- For every dollar saved or invested, match your children 50%. (similar to most 401k plans)
- Give your children a lump sum at the beginning of the month while explaining that they have to budget the money well because they will receive nothing else until the next month.
- The next time your children really want something, such as the latest and greatest video game console, tell them they have to get a job (any kind of job) and save for it.
- Every time you give your children cash for things like movie tickets, clothes, or a soda at the local convenience store, ask for the change!
- Have your children pay for some of their college expenses so they have a stake in their education. (one of my favorites!)
- Show how their money will exponentially grow over time through the power of compounding. (you can find many examples and calculators on the Internet)
- When devising your family budget for the year, ask your children to have some input regarding the projected amounts for expenses.

Being a good role model is vital when raising financially literate children. If your kids see you constantly spend money on frivolous items, they will likely do the same when they are on their own. If you live within your means, they are more likely to be frugal with their money and be able to invest for the long-term. In today's world, children who learn how to plan a budget, save, invest early, and manage their risk in their portfolios will live a less stressful and more satisfying life. We can all make a difference in this world by setting a high priority for financial literacy among our young citizens. The time is now to rise to the challenge in helping our kids grow up to become financially responsible in our communities across our great country. Good luck and happy parenting!

ABOUT THE AUTHOR

Michael Zisa received his Master's degree in Mathematics Education from The City College of New York and earned his Bachelor's degree in Business Management. After 5 ½ years as a high school Mathematics teacher in New York City, Mike had a rewarding career as a Senior Financial Analyst at Bank of America. He was also a Financial Advisor at Merrill Lynch before becoming an independent Financial Advisor. He holds the FINRA Series 7 and Series 66 securities registrations and offers financial planning services to his clients. Mike has been teaching Investment Management and Wealth Management at Pennsbury High School in Bucks County, PA since 2004, teaches a Business Communications class at a local college, and has developed financial education software curriculums for ISupportLearning, Inc. Additionally, he is a member of the Global Association of Teachers of Economics (GATE).